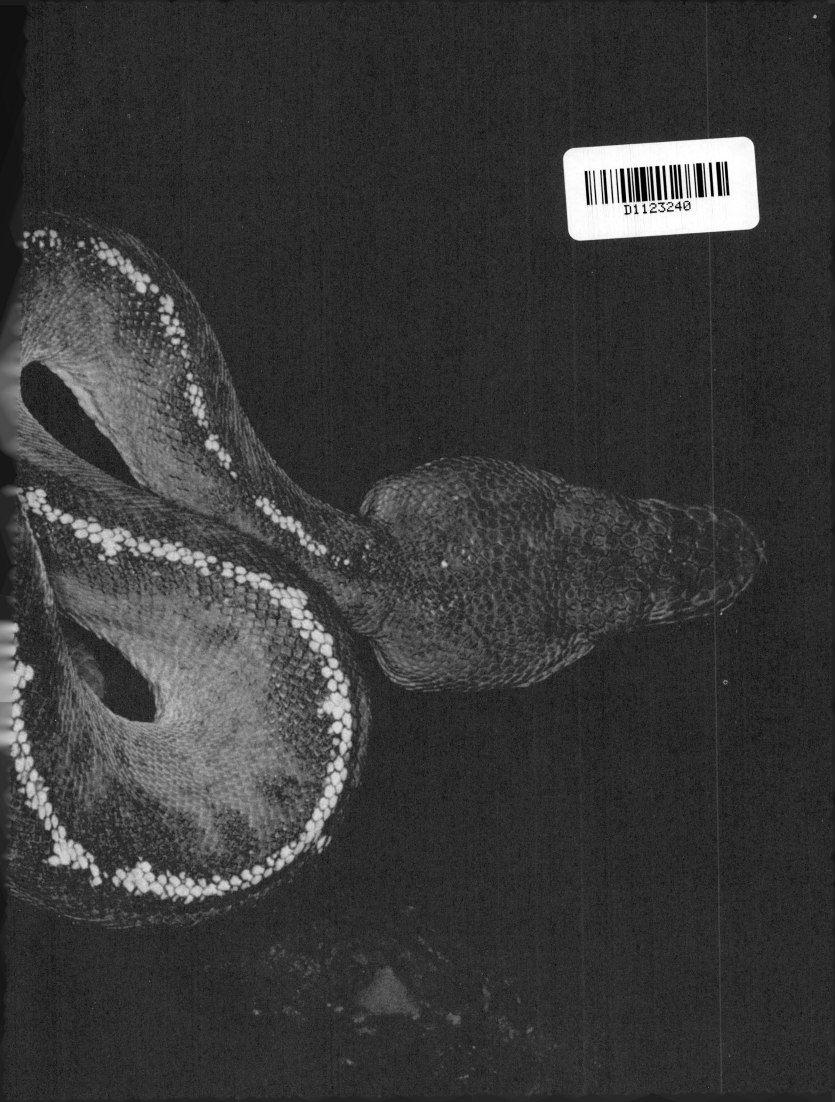

SNAKES, CROCODILES and LIZARDS

SNAKES, CROCODILES and LIZARDS

The World of reptiles and amphibians

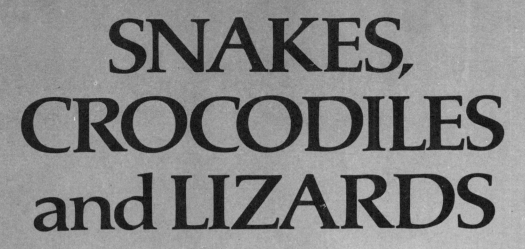

MAURICE BURTON DSc, FZS
Formerly Deputy Keeper of Zoology,
British Museum (Natural History)

With a foreword by
Angus d'A. Bellairs MA, DSc, MRCS
Professor of Vertebrate Morphology
in the University of London

ORBIS PUBLISHING · London

Contents

Frontispiece: Galapagos marine iguana
(William E. Ferguson)
Endpapers: Emerald green boa
(H. Chaumeton/Jacana)

© Istituto Geografico de Agostini, Novara 1973
English edition © Orbis Publishing Limited, London 1973
This edition published in 1978
Originally published as The World of Reptiles and Amphibians
Printed in Italy by IGDA, Novara
ISBN 0 85613 149 0

Foreword

by Angus d'A. Bellairs MA, DSc, MRCS
Professor of Vertebrate Morphology in the University of London

Some people tend to think of amphibians and reptiles as lowly, even repulsive creatures. In fact the great naturalist Linnaeus was guilty of this judgment when he described them as 'foul and loathsome animals', and added 'wherefore their Creator has not exerted his powers to make many of them'.

It must be admitted that creatures such as toads and salamanders, snakes and crocodiles may seem to lack the furry appeal of mammals or the charm of the active, ubiquitous birds. In temperate climes, at least, they play little part in man's everyday life, and they have long since lost the dominant position which they enjoyed in ages past. Nevertheless, these two classes of animals, the amphibians and reptiles, make up a very substantial proportion of the different kinds of vertebrate creatures found in the world today; they are, of course, particularly numerous in hot countries. Some of them, for example many frogs and lizards, are brightly coloured and beautiful. Snakes have a grace and fascination all of their own and the mystery of their sinuous progression confounded even the wisdom of King Solomon. Crocodiles are impressive reminders of the age of dinosaurs, of which animals they are the closest living relatives.

So far as man is concerned, amphibians are virtually harmless and some of them perform a useful function as predators on agricultural pests. One cannot deny, however, that some reptiles, crocodiles and certain snakes, are dangerous. Yet the toll of human life which they exact is negligible, compared with that levied by invertebrate and bacterial parasites, or indeed by man himself. We should also remember that reptiles are the victims as well as the killers of man; some species, such as sea turtles and giant tortoises have been ruthlessly exploited as a source of human food and their conservation is regarded as a matter of urgency by all those who are concerned with the welfare of animals in the modern world.

The science of amphibians and reptiles is known as herpetology, a word derived from the Greek herpeton, meaning a creeping thing. One of the most interesting branches of this subject is the study of the various adaptations which amphibians and reptiles show to their different ways of life. Many live in swamps, others in the sea, and some in almost waterless deserts; some live among the foliage of tropical rain-forests, while others burrow in the soil beneath. One has only to think of such amphibians as tree-frogs or the blind salamanders which live in cave pools, or of such reptiles as the geckos with their wonderful climbing feet to appreciate the versatility of these animals.

Dr. Burton has surveyed his subject with a discerning eye and gives a thoroughly readable and informative account of the classification and habits of amphibians and reptiles; no one who reads this beautifully illustrated book can fail to learn much about the fascinating creatures with which he deals. It will be a welcome addition to the library of every naturalist.

Index of Reptiles and Amphibians

Page references to photographs are printed in **heavy** type.

Introduction

About 350,000,000 years ago, the fossil record tells us, certain kinds of fishes took to crawling on the beds of rivers and swamps. They probably had lungs as well as gills and internal nostrils, and their paired fins were to some extent limb-like, enabling them to progress over the ground. The generally accepted theory is that these early fish were able to crawl overland when their pool, lake or river dried up, in order to find another source of water, using their lungs on these occasions somewhat in the manner of the lungfishes of today. It is probable that several orders of fishes had this propensity but all the fossil evidence points to the Rhipidistians as being the group from which amphibians arose. These freshwater, lobe-finned, carnivorous fish belong to the Temnospondyl labyrinthodonts. The oldest known amphibians are the Ichthyostegids. Their remains, found in the freshwater beds of Devonian rocks of Greenland, indicate that the creature was nearly a metre long, with an elongated, salamander-like body, a long tail with a fish-like fin and short legs, each bearing five toes.

The class Amphibia represents one of the five types of vertebrates or backboned animals, the other four being the fishes, reptiles, birds and mammals. The present day forms comprise the caecilians, the newts and salamanders, and the frogs and toads; all are cold-blooded. There are about 3,000 species living today, divided into three orders. The Gymnophiona or caecilians, of which there are only 158 species, are worm-like and without legs. The Caudata or tailed amphibians (newts and salamanders), also – but incorrectly – known as the Urodela, include about 300 species. The remaining species of frogs and toads, known collectively as tailless amphibians, comprise the order Anura, sometimes known as the Salientia (jumping amphibians).

The name Amphibia means 'double-life' and refers to the fact that, typically, these animals spend part of their lives in water and part on land. This double-living refers to the majority, there being some that never leave the water and some that never go near it.

In an evolutionary sense, as well as in appearance, amphibians are intermediate between fish and reptiles. The reptiles probably arose from an extinct group of anthracosaurian amphibians which first appeared about 320,000,000 years ago. Most amphibians can be distinguished from fish by their moist skin devoid of scales (caecilians are an exception), by a free living tadpole and by the presence of limbs; and from reptiles by the kind of eggs they lay. The amphibian egg lacks an outer protective shell; instead it is covered by several jelly-like envelopes.

West African caecilia
a legless amphibian wi
degenerate scales. It
is virtually blind and
burrows in the ground

AMPHIBIANS
Caecilians, salamanders and newts—tailed amphibians

(Below) great crested
or warty newt of
Europe; a male in
breeding dress

The skin of amphibians is made up of the usual two layers: an inner dermis and an outer epidermis; the latter is made up of dead cells which, on land, help to prevent loss of moisture and it is this layer that is cast as the amphibian grows. The skin is kept moist by mucous glands. This is what makes a frog's skin slimy to the touch. In tree frogs special mucous glands on the toes, secreting a sticky substance, help them cling to vertical surfaces. There may be poison glands in the skin, which give out a milky fluid, as in the European common toad; many amphibians that possess these are brightly coloured.

The brilliant colours possessed by many amphibians result from three kind of pigment cells, or chromatophores, in the skin. It is by the expansion and contraction of these that some amphibians, such as tree frogs, can change colour quickly.

The skin of amphibians also plays a major role in respiration. The tailed frog *Ascaphus truei,* living in the fast-flowing streams of British Columbia, Washington and Oregon, that are rich in dissolved oxygen, has very small lungs and breathes mainly through the skin. The lungless salamanders, having no lungs or gills, breathe entirely through the skin. Other amphibians use the skin for respiration to a greater or lesser degree, according to the species, and many also breathe through the skin lining the mouth.

One reason for this use of the skin is that the lungs, when present, cannot be inflated and deflated by movements of the ribs. Although some amphibians have ribs they do not have a flexible rib cage. Instead the floor of the mouth is raised and lowered and the nostrils are alternately closed and opened, forcing the air into the lungs. The air

then escapes, forced out by the elastic nature of the lungs. This is an inefficient method, since only a mouthful of air can enter the lungs at a time.

Although many lower animals make sounds, for example some insects and many fishes, they do so by other means than the use of vocal cords. In ascending the animal scale, a true voice is first met in the amphibians, but not in all. The caecilians, salamanders and newts have no vocal chords, although some make faint squeaks. Where true vocalizations occur in frogs and toads, they are caused by air being forced backwards and forwards across the vocal cords, with the mouth and nostrils closed, which is why frogs and toads can croak under water.

Usually only males call and they do so with sounds distinctive for the species. Barking frogs ranging from Texas to Mexico, sound at a distance like dogs barking; others have calls like tinkling bells or various musical sounds. When alarmed or seized by a predator, some frogs squeal or scream with the mouth wide open.

Since salamanders do not vocalize it is not surprising that they have no ear-drum, but they can detect vibrations transmitted through the bones of the fore-legs to the skull. In most frogs and toads the ear-drum is large and visible as a circular area of thin skin just behind the eye.

The tongue plays no part in the vocalizations. Most amphibians have a tongue, exceptions being certain toads that spend all of their time in water. Some salamanders living wholly in water have only a fleshy fold in the floor of the mouth. The usual pattern is for the tongue to be attached to the floor of the front part of the mouth, the main part being folded back. It is muscular and can be flicked out rapidly for the capture of prey,

this being assisted by glands in the mouth that secrete a sticky fluid.

Most amphibians are sight-animals. The caecilians are blind and some salamanders living in caves are nearly so. Their eyes are degenerate. In all others the eyes are a prominent feature, especially in nocturnal species. The eyes are high up on the head in aquatic forms and look like glistening jewels. They are, however, limited in performance and the sight is deficient as compared with that of most higher animals. In higher animals, including humans, the eye receives the light rays but the processing of information is carried out in the brain. In amphibians much of the processing takes place in the retina itself, which means that responses to visual objects are simple. A frog does not see an insect in detail but reacts to anything that moves and has a curved front, two qualities applicable to a live insect.

Amphibians, being cold-blooded, become lethargic at low temperatures and in temperate regions hibernate in the ground or on mud at the bottom of water. They cease to feed and breathe entirely through the skin. Nevertheless they often emerge to breed in the early part of the year, when temperatures are comparatively low.

Breeding is usually limited to one part of the year which varies in different regions and is often closely linked with the climate. In temperate regions breeding is at the end of winter or in early spring, in the tropics it generally starts with a rainy season. The spadefoot toads of North America and the water-holding frogs of Australia breed in temporary pools formed after rainstorms in the desert regions where rains are infrequent.

In tailed amphibians the courtship is limited to the male placing himself alongside the female, or crosswise in front of her, and beating the water gently with his tail. Similar tail-beating is used by some fishes for wooing or for aggression, and the vibrations set up are supposed to have an appropriate effect on the female. The fact that some male newts put on breeding colours at this time, or develop a high crest along the back and tail, suggests that all these things are stimulants to the female. Although internal fertilization is practised by all reptiles it is relatively unusual in amphibians. In the salamanders and newts there is no coition, the male simply deposits his sperm in capsules, or spermatophores and the female moves over a spermatophore until she is able to pick it up with the lips of her cloaca (the common exit in lower vertebrates for waste matter and reproductive products). In a few primitive salamanders the male sheds his sperm direct into the water and fertilization is external.

In the tailless amphibians fertilization of the eggs occurs outside the female's body. They use an amplexus (sexual coupling) in mating. The male clings to the female's back until she lays her eggs into the water. He then releases his sperm to fertilize them. There is little ceremony in it. The males' croaking attracts the females to the water, where amplexus takes place and when the female is spent she may give a low grunt, or otherwise indicate that the male should depart. Exceptions to the generally adopted internal fertilization are found in the caecilians which have an intromittant organ and in the primitive tailed frog *Ascaphus*, where the 'tail', which is an external cloaca, is used by the male to introduce sperm into the female.

The eggs are enclosed in thick layers of jelly surrounding them individually or in a mass. The spawn, as the whole mass is called, may be in clumps or in strings or the eggs may be laid singly. The number of eggs laid by each female varies from one in a Cuban species to as many as 35,000 in others.

The larvae of tailed amphibians look like miniature adults except for feather-like, external gills on the sides of the head. Most tailless amphibians are tadpoles or pollywogs to begin with and these change into tiny replicas of the adults after a complicated metamorphosis. The interval between egg-laying and hatching may be from two days, in the case of spadefoot toads that lay in temporary pools, to 14 days or more. Hurter's spadefoot *Scaphiophus hurteri* may take 12 to 40 days. After that anything up to three months may elapse before the change into a froglet or toadlet.

As a rule, the tadpoles are at first vegetarian, clinging to and feeding on water plants by holding on with the lips. They have external feathery gills. Later, they change to a carnivorous diet and correlated with this the intestine becomes shorter. At the same time lungs begin to develop, then the hind limbs start to grow out, the gills become covered with a fold of skin, and the front legs begin to grow within the fold. Finally the tail is absorbed, but this is a slow process and often the tail is still relatively long when the metamorphosing frog or toad leaves the water for dry land.

In frogs and toads that breed on land there is a trend towards elimination of a free living larval stage, and development into adult form is completed within the egg. An extreme condition occurs in the African *Nectophrynoides* where miniature adults are born alive.

It takes one to four years, depending on the species, for an amphibian to reach sexual maturity. Life expectancy in the wild is probably short, but the potential life-span is 30 to 40 years, judging by records of amphibians in captivity.

*ft) well-grown larva
he European smooth
t, showing the pink,
hery gills typical
ewts of the family
amandridae*

*ges 6–7) axolotl, the
enous or permanent
a of the Mexican
mander, with the
cal form and gills
he salamander family*

5

There may appear to be a considerable gulf between the general appearance of amphibians and reptiles but in both groups limbless forms occur. The Latin *caecilia* referred to a kind of lizard, and *caecitas* means blindness. The caecilians possess no limbs or even limb-girdles and due to the habit of burrowing head first, the bones of the skull are relatively stout. The smallest are 112 mm long, the largest 140 cm, and none is more than 25 mm in diameter. They are slim, worm-like creatures that live in damp places in warm-temperate regions. Their skin is moist from mucus-secreting glands but many have minute scales sunk in the skin, which however are quite unlike the epidermal scales of reptiles. There is a single sensory tentacle close to the eye connected with Jacobson's organ – a kind of smell-taste organ – in the nasal cavity. They are blind and earless but receive vibrations through the bone of the lower jaw. Their left lung is small, the right one is large and long, and they also breathe through the skin.

Some female caecilians lay eggs from which hatch free-swimming larvae with external gills. At least one species lays eggs in which the larvae develop and shed their gills before hatching. In other species the eggs are retained within the female body and develop there, while yet other species bear living young, the egg-capsule rupturing early so that the young develop outside it – but within the maternal body.

Although superficially caecilians look quite different from other amphibians such as salamanders, newts, frogs and toads they all have numerous features in common that suggest a common ancestry.

The large salamanders of the family Cryptobranchidae look more like what you would expect of ancestral amphibians. This family contains the real giants among salamanders – the Japanese giant salamander *Andrias japonicus*, 1·5 m long, the Chinese giant salamander, 1 m long, and the related hellbender of the United States which is 64 cm long. The Asian species have weak limbs and live in mountain streams. The Cryptobranchidae have a poor sense of hearing but as in most aquatic amphibians and the larvae of terrestrial amphibians, they have lateral line organs along the flanks comparable with those of fishes. These seem to be sensitive to vibrations in the water. *Andrias* also has an unusual, probably primitive, method of reproduction. The females lay twin sacs of eggs, gluing them to a rock surface. The male pushes her aside with his hind legs so freeing her from the sacs, then sheds his sperm over them to fertilize the eggs.

The Pacific giant salamander *Dicamptodon*

(Above) the egg of the palmate newt has developed into the early larva but is still enclosed in an Elodea *leaf*

(Top left) eggs of the palmate newt, each in a folded leaf of the waterweed Elodea

(Left) larva of the palmate newt, now hatched and hanging by its mouth from a leaf of Elodea

ensatus of the coastal forests from British Columbia to California is 30 cm long. It belongs to the same family as the mole salamanders, of which there are about 15 species, all North American. Most of them lay their eggs in the water and once breeding is finished they leave the water, disappearing into the grass or other herbage and are rarely seen again until the following spring.

The Pacific giant salamander is remarkable for making a low bark or scream when disturbed. One of the mole salamanders is famous but for an entirely different reason. It is *Ambystoma mexicanum* and it lives in lakes around Mexico City. While most species of *Ambystoma* progress from larva to adult in the normal way, a *mexicanum* often fails to turn into an adult yet is able to breed in larval state; it is known as the axolotl.

Neoteny (the state of sexual maturity without achieving adult form) is found sporadically in several species of salamanders and newts. This retarded development can be counteracted by administering extract of thyroid.

The original salamander was the fire salamander of Europe, about which has grown the legend that it can pass through fire unharmed. It, with other salamanders and newts, comprises the family Salamandridae. These are the most numerous of the tailed amphibians. The difference between a newt and a salamander is largely one of etymology. In Middle English the tailed amphibians found living in English ponds and streams were called *ewt* or *eft*. In time 'an ewt' became 'a newt'.

The first newt to be studied in detail was the European smooth newt *Triturus vulgaris*. The male is 11 cm long, the female slightly longer. It

lives on land but takes to water for the breeding season. Its colour is brown to olive, sometimes reddish, with dark blotches which are smaller in the female; the underside is white to yellow or rose. In the breeding season the fin running along the back and round the tail becomes enlarged and frilled and is coloured red along the edges, with a blue border in the male.

Breeding follows the pattern described on page 5. After fertilization the female lays her eggs singly on the undersides of leaves of water plants. As each egg is laid the female, using the toes of the hind feet, wraps the leaf around it, the stickiness of the egg keeping the leaf gummed to it. The eggs hatch in two weeks. The larvae are miniatures of the adults except for three feathery gills on each side of the head. They change to adult form in three months. Other common European newts are the great crested or warty newt *T. cristatus*, 17 cm or more long, and the palmate newt *T. helveticus*, 10 cm long with webbed hind feet.

The breeding of the European spotted salamander, or fire salamander, *Salamandra salamandra*, follows similar lines to that of the newts except that the male makes a clumsy attempt to embrace the female, clambering onto her back, and the young are born alive. In the alpine salamander *S. atra*, which is glossy black with yellow markings, mating is on land and the young are born alive without gills.

Although we tend to think of newts and salamanders as spending part of their time on land and part in water, there is considerable variation in this. The alpine salamander hardly ever enters water. The spotted salamander only enters shallow water – and then only the female – to give

(Above left) pair of palmate newts, the male approaching the female from above

(Above right) eastern mud salamander Pseudotriton montanus montanus, *one of the many lungless salamanders of North America that breathe entirely through the skin*

10

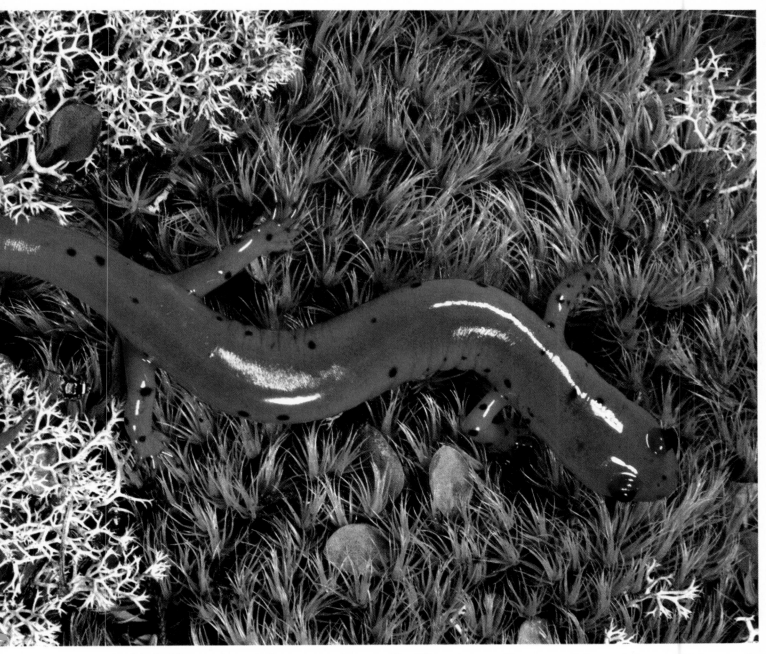

birth. The great crested newt spends part of its life in water and part on land, and so do the smooth, palmate and alpine newts although they spend more time on land.

In the eastern United States the red-spotted newt *Notopthalmus viridescens* loses its gills at three months of age and comes on land. There it remains for the next three to four years, when it is known as the red eft. It is up to 7·5 cm long, bright orange-red with two rows of vermilion spots ringed in black. At the end of this stage it returns to water to become adult, its colour then changing to olive-green, greenish-brown or yellow-brown. Some individuals, by contrast, remain in the water all the time.

The California newt *Taricha torosa,* comes on land mainly when the ponds dry out, yet its larva must come out on land at the metamorphosis and drowns if prevented from doing so. This newt is unusual also in its courtship. The males reach the breeding ponds first and as each female arrives she is surrounded by a milling crowd of males, one of which succeeds in clambering onto her back and clasps her body behind the forelegs. Then he rubs his cloaca on her back and strokes her head with his chin. A gland on his chin apparently stimulates her to breeding condition. After that he deposits his spermatophore on the bottom of the pond for her to pick up in the usual way.

The fire salamander, as well as some newts in Europe, has been feared for alleged poisonous properties. This is to some extent justified in the fire salamander which secretes a highly distasteful milky fluid from glands on the skin. Its colours – yellow and black, occasionally red and black in Iberian populations – advertise this to likely predators, for these two colours, and red, are the usual 'warning colours'. The red eft also has toxic glands giving out a secretion that irritates the mucus lining of the mouth of any animal seeking to eat it. So we find this amphibian, while on land, making little attempt to hide. Moreover, when the time comes for individuals to return to water they tend to gather at one spot and move in a group. The colours of the mass probably present an even greater deterrent.

The rough-skin newt *Taricha granulosa*, of the Pacific coast of North America feigns dead in an almost acrobatic way. When disturbed it bends its head and tail upwards until the two nearly touch. The tip of the tail becomes tightly-coiled and the orange belly is exposed to view. At the same time the legs are stretched stiffly outwards, the eyes recede into their sockets and the lids close.

The amphiumas, salamanders of the family Amphiumidae, defend themselves by biting with their sharp teeth. There are three species, all North American. The largest, the two-toed amphiuma *Amphiuma means,* is eel-like, up to 1 m long, and is known as the Congo eel. It lives in rivers and streams of the south-eastern United States, where it feeds on crayfishes, snails and other small animals. It has legs but these are minute.

In North America are many species of lungless salamanders which, except as larvae, have no gills either and breathe through their skin. Several of them have unusual methods of protection. The dusky salamander *Desmognathus fuscus,* of eastern North America, slow-moving and beset by many enemies, progresses by leaps when alarmed. The slimy salamander *Plethodon glutinosus* gives out a thick glue from its skin which is non-toxic. The four-toed salamander *Hemidactylium scutatum* can throw off its tail, like a lizard, to

baffle a pursuer. The arboreal salamander *Aneides lugubris* not only bites – and the female will defend her eggs – but has been known to climb trees to a height of 20 m.

Several lungless salamanders have gone to live in caves or underground waters, both in North America and Europe. One, the cave salamander *Eurycea lucifuga,* lives in limestone caves from Virginia to Oklahoma. The more famous cave-dweller is the olm *Proteus anguinus,* an unusual salamander, of the caverns of Carniola, Carinthia and Dalmatia in southern Europe. It is 30 cm long, white to pink with carmine gills, the eyes are covered with skin, and it lives in the total darkness of the caves. The olm is neotenous, and belongs to the family Proteidae in which is included the mud puppy *Necturus maculosus of* North America, another neotenous amphibian. The mud puppy lives in muddy or weedy lakes or ponds, coming out at night to feed on fish, snails and insects. The Sirenidae, another family, are the neotenous sirens of North America. They live all their lives in water, have permanent gills, feeble legs and a reduced number of toes, yet will sometimes crawl out on land. Should a siren's pond dry out, it will encase itself in a cocoon of mud and become dry while its gills shrivel. When the pond again fills with water, even after several weeks, the siren's skin becomes moist again and its gills swell to their former size.

(Below left) adult Mexican salamander. It lives on land, returning to water to breed

(Below) European spotted salamander Salamandra salamandra, *the fire salamander of legend, stalking an earthworm*

Toads and Frogs—tailless amphibians

The Anura, the order to which the frogs and toads belong is related to a fossil known as *Triadobatrachus* (formerly called *Protobatrachus*) that occurred 230,000,000 years ago in Madagascar. It had a skull somewhat similar to that of present day frogs but many features of its limb bones and backbone as well as the presence of a tail are quite unlike those of any modern tailless amphibians. Even as much as 130,000,000 years ago there were frogs and toads very like those living today.

In present day frogs and toads the tail is resorbed during metamorphosis, the bones of the forearm are fused and there are fewer vertebrae. The long legs of modern frogs are largely due to an elongation of the ankle, and they give these animals good leaping powers. The North American bullfrog *Rana catesbeiana*, for example, can leap nine times its own body length. The sharp-nosed frog *Ptychadena oxyrhyncha*, much smaller than the bullfrog, can cover 40 times its own length.

The smallest anuran is believed to be the Cuban toad *Sminthillus limbatus*, 12 mm long, and the largest *Conrana goliath* of the Cameroon region, 300 mm long.

The classification of the Anura has always been difficult for it is based principally on a combination of features of the skeleton, muscles and life history. No single character can be relied upon to separate one group from another and the non-specialist inevitably encounters difficulties in identifying the family to which an anuran belongs.

Toads, strictly speaking, are those belonging to one family only, the Bufonidae, but the name tends to be used indiscriminately. An example of this is seen in the family Pipidae, usually called tongueless frogs. The best known member is the Surinam toad *Pipa pipa*. Like all members of the family the Surinam toad lives entirely or almost entirely in water and feeds by searching the mud with long slender toes on the forelegs, seizing any small animal, dead or alive, to cram into its mouth. The toad itself is flattened and black, so that it is hard to see as it lies on mud. Even the eyes do not betray it, they are so small. The long front toes have star-shaped clusters of glandular filaments at their tips, highly sensitive touch-

*(Left) tadpole of the European common toad soon after the
hind-legs have appeared*

*(Below left) African clawed toad in its natural element,
showing the large webbed hind feet*

*(Below) midwife toad, curiously misnamed since it is the male
that looks after the eggs*

organs for searching in mud.

Another peculiarity is in the breeding. The female lays her eggs while in an upside down position in the water and with the male attached to her. As she rights herself the eggs roll over her back into pits and the male's body prevents the eggs from falling off into the water. When 60 or so have been thus placed he swims away and the skin of the female's back grows over the eggs. In time the eggs hatch and lids pop up from the site of each of them and out comes a froglet.

The African clawed frog *Xenopus laevis*, an-

(Above) two stages in the metamorphosis of the African clawed toads; on the left the larva or tadpole, and above it the toadlet into which it will turn

(Above right) pixie toad of East Africa Pyxicephalus delalandii *seen here gulping a sausage fly*

(Right) metamorphosing toadlets of pixie toad in mud

other member of the family, sometimes comes on land. Three of its slender 'fingers' bear claws. It breeds in the normal way, and its claim to fame is that it was the first amphibian used for pregnancy tests. Injected with urine from a woman the female clawed frog would start to lay if the woman were pregnant. Later it was found that most female frogs react in this way.

The next family, the Discoglossidae, is characterized by having a round disk-like tongue, and it contains two well-known types: the fire-bellied toad *Bombina bombina* and the midwife toad *Alytes obstetricans*. The fire-belly is orange on its underside and its skin is poisonous. When alarmed it turns onto its back, its fire-belly acting as a warning signal to enemies that it is unpleasant to taste.

The midwife toad lays her eggs in strings. The male pushes his legs through the tangled string

(Far left) European common toads in amplexus, as the mating embrace is called. The spawn is laid in long strings

(Left) Oriental fire-bellied toad Bombina orientalis *exposing its orange underside as a warning*

(Left) Plains spadefoot toad Scaphiophus bombifrons *of the Great Plains of the United States*

Malayan toad Bufo asper *feeds on insects that eat the guano of bats roosting in the Batu caves*

and retires to his damp burrow. At night he comes out to feed and also to go to water where he dips the eggs to moisten them.

Spadefoots, or spadefoot toads (some of them are called frogs!) of the family Pelobatidae, have a horny crescent-shaped 'spade' on the side of each hind foot. The animal squats on the ground, seemingly motionless, and slowly sinks into the ground. It has been shovelling earth aside, unseen, with its hind feet. In dry weather spadefoots may burrow a metre or more. By being burrowers, and by coming out mainly at night or on wet days, they avoid being dried up as well as escaping enemies. In fact, they conceal themselves so well that people living in the same locality may not be aware of their presence.

These amphibians are found over much of the northern hemisphere. In Europe the garlic toad *Pelobates fuscus* gives out a skin secretion smelling like garlic when roughly handled. This is stronger in the male than the female. The spadefoots of eastern and south-western United States look and behave like the garlic toad but have specialities as larvae. Their eggs hatch in two days and the larvae can change to froglets within two to six weeks after that. Everything depends on the food supply, and this leads to co-operative behaviour in the larvae. They feed on organic particles in the water. When water is in short supply the tadpoles bunch together and as they swim the combined action of their tails stirs up the mud, including food matter. Should the level of a pond drop dangerously they will group, and the swirl from their lashing tails scoops a basin in the mud into which water drains. If all else fails the group indulges in cannibalism.

One spadefoot toad, the Asiatic horned frog *Megophrys monticola,* is believed because of its wide mouth and strong jaws to be more than usually cannibalistic when adult.

The Mexican burrowing toad *Rhinophrynus dorsalis,* 63 mm long, of the family Rhinophrynidae, is a toothless creature that burrows into anthills. The hind feet are webbed but the inner toe has a hard horny spade. The tongue is rooted in the back of the mouth and the toad can stick it out as can mammals.

The barking frog *Eleutherodactylus augusti,* ranging from Texas to Mexico, looks like a toad and has the toad habit of blowing itself up when alarmed. Its voice is like the distant barking of a dog. It is related to the greenhouse frog *E.*

ricordi planirostris, a native of the south-eastern United States that is frequently found in greenhouses where it lays its eggs in damp crevices. Both belong to the Leptodactylidae, frogs common in tropical America, South Africa and in Australia. The High Andean aquatic forms are especially large, and pugnacity seems to be a feature of several members of the family, which includes several horned toads.

The 'horns' are merely triangular, spine-like processes of skin, one over each eye. Wied's frog *Ceratophyrs varia*, which comes from Brazil, is a pugnacious frog with a shield of bone protecting its back and head. Other horned frogs (or toads) have bony shields, wide mouths, with jaws like steel traps armed with sharp teeth, and they tend to have variegated colour patterns. In Guenther's frog *E. guentheri* these last are particularly variable. One individual may have a dark cross on

(Right) Colombian horned frog Ceratophrys calcarata *with its tongue bulging as it tries to swallow another frog*

(Pages 22–3) the elephant hawk moth caterpillar can make itself look like a miniature snake, so the toad about to eat it changes its mind and blows itself up as it would on meeting a snake

20

the back, another dark lines down the flanks, another a chequered pattern of light and dark. These and other variants may turn up in a single brood.

There is also Guenther's horned frog *Ceratophrys appendiculata* which has a long spike of skin on its nose, looking like a sting. In the Argentine another horned frog *C. ornata* has an evil reputation; it is said to bite the lip of a grazing horse, causing its death. This idea arose from the frog's habit of attacking animals larger than itself.

The leptodactylid frogs of Australia include some of the water-holding amphibians. In times of drought the Aborigines are said to locate these frogs which bury themselves in the sandy earth, dig them out, squeeze them and catch the water in their mouths that the frogs give out. One of the best known is the holy cross frog or catholic frog *Notaden bennetti*. The name is from a dark cross on its back. In general, water-holding frogs live in deserts, burrow well into the soil when a drought begins and do not come out until the next rains.

Even in the hottest deserts moisture may be found at 20 to 30 cm below the surface. The skin of any tailless amphibian can readily give up or take in moisture. A frog in temperate regions can lose 45 per cent of its body water and survive, replenishing it when water is available, without drinking. The water-holding frogs have especially large bladders for storing water and by burrowing deep make sure they lose none. Another way they ensure water retention is by shedding a layer of skin, one cell thick, that forms a cocoon all around the frog, separated from it except at the nostrils. Water accumulates between the cocoon and the skin, inhibiting further loss from the body.

The true toads (Bufonidae) number 340 species and occur in all temperate and tropical regions except for Madagascar, Australasia and the oceanic islands (where the marine toad was introduced – see page 28). They have plump bodies and short legs. If they hop it is without the agility of frogs, and being slow-moving they need extra protection; this is supplied in most toads by a conspicuous parotoid gland behind each eye which emits an irritating poison. Smaller, similar glands may be found in 'warts' elsewhere on the body but some toads lack both parotoid and other conspicuous glands. A dog even touching a toad with its lips shows acute signs of distress with saliva streaming down from its mouth.

Defence posture of a common European toad; it blows itself up and raises itself on all four legs

(Above) European tree frogs showing their acrobatic skill

(Left) male marine toad with throat sac distended, calling to the female in the breeding season

True toads usually have a strong homing ability. Each individual has its favoured niche, among grass or stones, and returns to it daily after a foraging expedition. The European common toad and others also visit the same ponds each year for breeding, as do frogs. The toads, however, follow traditional routes on these migrations and where these cross main roads, now busy with traffic, there are heavy casualties. There has long been speculation about how the toads find their way to the ponds. It now seems likely that they use celestial navigation – by the stars by night and the sun by day.

One reason why toads are more vulnerable than frogs on the roads is that their locomotion is more laboured and they cannot jump out of the way. But they have an alternative method of escape from enemies: they react to danger by blowing themselves up with air and raising themselves on stiff legs. A snake that includes toads in its diet sometimes finds it impossible to get a grasp on the victim with its mouth when the toad is inflated.

Toads, more so than frogs perhaps, are the friends of gardeners and farmers because of the insects they consume. They have enormous appetites and one species especially has been made use of for this reason – the marine toad *Bufo marinus,* of tropical America. Sugar cane from eastern Asia was taken to warm countries around the world and with it went the grey cane beetle, the larvae of which attack its roots. The marine toad, so named because it was first noticed near the coast, feeds on the beetle. In an effort to control the beetle the toad was introduced into Florida, Bermuda, many Caribbean islands, Hawaii, New Guinea and Australia. In the main it failed to control the beetle, but became well settled in its new homes. The marine toad is said to be the most poisonous of all toads and animals in its new homes soon learn to leave it alone. Although so poisonous to its enemies, it can also blow itself up in self-protection. The female can lay 35,000 eggs a year, giving a high potential for building up numbers. Other large toads lay similar numbers, and on the whole egg production is correlated with size. The tiny Cuban toad *Sminthillus limbatus,* lays only one egg a year.

There are some toads known as running toads that can move more rapidly than the normal kind. One such is the natterjack of Europe *Bufo calamita.* Small, with short legs, it runs in short spurts almost like a mouse, and in the dusk could be mistaken for one. Even so, it also uses the blowing-up trick against enemies. Another runner is Rose's toad *B. rosei,* of the mountain slopes above Cape Town, South Africa. Only 25 mm long, it cannot jump more than that length, but can run quite fast.

In the remarkable Darwin's frog (family Rhinodermatidae) of South America, the male uses its vocal sacs as a nursery. These sacs are enormously enlarged, reaching from the groin along the flanks to the chin. Each female lays 20 to 30 eggs. Several males gather round and guard the eggs for 10 to 20 days, until they are about to hatch. Then each male takes several into his mouth. They pass into the vocal sacs where the larvae spend the vulnerable first part of their lives fully protected.

In many species of frogs the glands that keep the skin moist are toxic, especially to other frogs. For example, the pickerel frog *Rana palustris* of North America is lethal to frogs of other species. Naturalists collecting the frogs *Hyla vasta* in the West Indies and *Phrynomerus bifasciatus* in Africa have suffered from rashes on their hands.

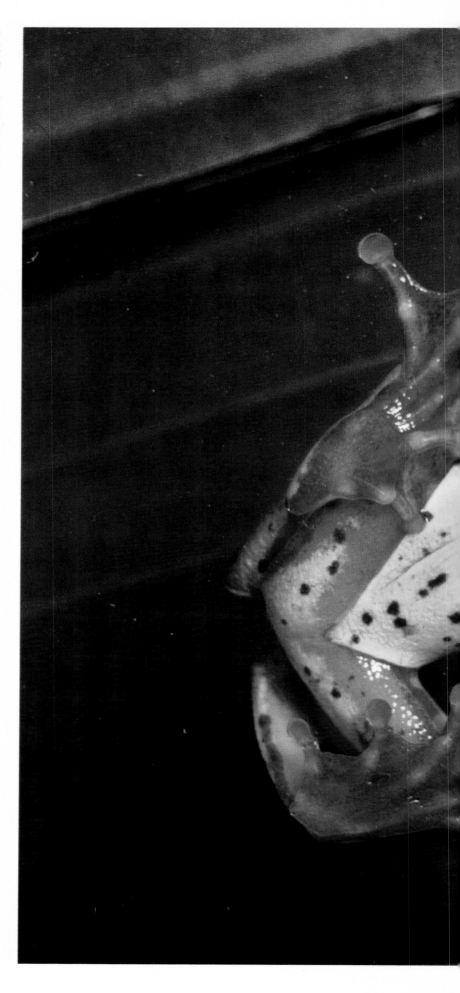

Reed frog seen from underneath as it clings to a vertical pane of glass with the aid of the expanded tips of its toes

Probably the most toxic are the arrow-poison frogs of South America, brightly coloured species of the genera *Dendrobates* and *Phyllobates* of the family Ranidae. The local Indians hold the frog spitted on a stick over a fire and collect fluid oozing from the skin. This is allowed to ferment and arrows tipped with it are used to capture food animals.

Atelopus frogs of the family Bufonidae, common in Central and South America, are also poisonous. When alarmed, one species *Atelopus stelzneri* of Uruguay, jet-black with bright orange feet, will bend its head and legs sharply upwards, exposing the orange surfaces as if in warning to would-be predators. The European common frog *Rana temporaria* when alarmed will, on occasion, flatten itself on the ground and bring its forefeet over its eyes, as if protecting

(Above) Mascarene frog showing how well the green stripe down the back camouflages it in grass

(Right) male reed frog blowing out his throat sac to an enormous balloon to make sounds out of proportion to his size

30

bove) tadpoles of the ropean common frog h one (bottom left) ning into a froglet

Tree frogs, and some other tailless amphibians, are such masters of concealment partly because of their colours and partly because they are largely nocturnal. This has meant that some species are known better by their voices than by their appearance. This quality is epitomized by the tree frog *Hyla annectens,* of China, which is known to the local people as 'bamboo spirit'. It lives in bamboo clumps giving frequent calls but only the most persistent searcher is rewarded by sight of it. Most of the time it is heard but not seen.

The reason why the Chinese tree frog and others have proved so elusive is that their calls carry so far and tend to have a ventriloquial quality like those of birds, whose calls they often resemble. When frogs or toads assemble in ponds it is easy to pin-point their position as a group although not always to locate them as individuals. When, as with many tree frogs, single individuals are calling, they are hard to find. The secret of the carrying power lies in the vocal sacs; a pair of cavities in the cheeks of a frog or toad, or a single cavity in the throat, that can be distended. They are, by the nature of things, most in evidence at the breeding season, when they protrude enormously from the sides of the head or the throat and act as resonators.

The calls themselves are varied: the spring peeper *H. crucifer* of eastern North America sounds like sleigh bells, the Cuban tree frog *H. septentrionalis* snores, while the golden tree frog *H. aurea* of Australia sounds like stonemasons at work with chisel and hammer.

In their breeding habits there is equal diversity. Most tree frogs go to water to breed in the usual way but Rohde's tree frog *Phyllomedusa rohdei* glues its eggs to the undersides of leaves overhanging water, the larvae dropping into the water in the early tadpole stage. Some tree frogs make mud nests in shallows at the margins of ponds, each nest being surrounded by a rampart of mud with a pit at the centre.

The most remarkable is the marsupial frog *Gastrotheca ovifera.* As the female lays her eggs the male, after fertilizing them, eases them up with his hind feet into a pouch covering the whole of her back. The opening of the pouch is at the lower end of her back. Only a few large eggs are laid and when in the pouch they can be seen as a series of rounded lumps. When the young have reached the froglet stage, the female lifts her hind foot and with one toe raises the lip of the slit-like opening to the pouch and the froglets come out.

The ghost frogs *Heleophryne* are the only African members of a family (Leptodactylidae) that is otherwise restricted to the Americas and Australasia. Only three species of *Heleophryne*

them from a would-be attacker. The reason for this is, however, not apparent. These contortions remind us that frogs and toads as a whole are not noted for their athletic or acrobatic prowess.

The tree frogs (Hylidae) form a sharp contrast, showing themselves to be trapeze artists – if provided with a trapeze. Normally living in shrubs and trees, they show considerable agility. This is due largely to the sticky tips of the toes being expanded and acting as suckers. Some species have in addition a sucker on the belly, which aids their clinging to vertical surfaces, a feature found also in frogs that live near or in mountain streams and cling to the vertical surfaces of rocks.

There are 500 species of tree frogs distributed over every continent and living up to 5,000 m above sea-level. They are mainly green, matching the foliage, but often there are brightly-coloured patches exposed as they leap through the air. These are called flash colours and are exposed only while the frog is in movement; they are hidden when the legs are folded. To a predator it is confusing – or this is the assumption – because at one moment the bright colours flash, making their possessor stand out and the next moment the frog seemingly has vanished.

The high incidence of green is underlined by the number of different tree frogs in Europe, Asia and North America that are called green frogs. Yet some tree frogs are capable of a wide range of rapid colour-changes according to changes in the intensity of light and other circumstances. But the most colourful features of tree frogs is their eyes and the same could be said of other amphibians . . . 'the toad, ugly and venomous, wears yet a precious jewel in its head' *(As you like it).*

Left) male American ree frog Hyla ersicolor with its hroat sac blown out alling with a loud trill, which it does at intervals f about half a minute

are known and they are confined to forests and swift mountain streams in South Africa. Their tadpoles are perfectly adapted to living in fast currents. Their heads and bodies are greatly flattened and they cling to the submerged rocks by means of an enormous oral sucker under the head, and browse the film of algae.

Tadpoles often appear larger than the froglets they turn into at metamorphosis. From its first discovery a century or so ago, *Pseudis paradoxa* (family Pseudidae), has been called the paradoxical frog. It lives in South America. The adult is only 7·5 cm long but the fully-grown tadpole is 25 cm, over three times this length. So there is a reduction in the size of the internal organs, instead of the usual increase with metamorphosis.

We can visualize the tailless amphibians as consisting of three large families with a number of small families in orbit around them. These smaller families are needed to contain species with anatomical or behavioural peculiarities, so that they stand outside the main families. The three main families are the true toads (Bufonidae), the tree frogs (Hylidae) already dealt with, and the Ranidae or true frogs.

The Ranidae, very rich in species, are found in all temperate and tropical regions except southern Australia and New Zealand. When Linnaeus wrote his *Systema Naturae*, in the mid-18th century, in which he set forth his classification of the animal kingdom, he put all the amphibians known to him under the heading Rana, which he described as having a tetrapodal body, naked and without a tail.

It was with the muscles of a European frog's leg that Galvani in the 18th century demonstrated

True frogs breed in shallow lakes or swamps. Some disperse over the surrounding countryside outside the breeding season, others keep near water all the time and seek safety by diving into it. They have long hind legs and jump well. They feed mainly on insects caught with the sticky tongue but the larger species will swallow such prey as mice, the smaller rats and the young of water birds.

A female frog may lay around 5,000 eggs and a fair-sized pond will be used by hundreds of breeding females. The metamorphosing tadpoles usually emerge onto land about the same time, and should there be a shower of rain about this time they erupt from the pond more or less all at once. This may be one of the reasons why 'Rains of Frogs' have so often been reported. At the same time it is by no means certain that tiny froglets may not at times be carried up in waterspouts and cascaded to earth some distance away.

Some true frogs lay their eggs on land. Members of the genus *Platymantis*, living in Borneo and New Guinea, lay their eggs in damp soil and the frog develops within the egg capsule. *Hemisus marmoratus* of tropical Africa lays its eggs in a small cavity in the bank of a pool above water level. Rattray's frog *Anhydrophryne rattrayi* lays its eggs in holes in the ground. The tadpoles remain in the holes in the liquefied jelly of the eggs.

These frogs, and others with similar egg-laying habits, need moisture for the eggs to develop, but water drowns them. The larvae pass the tadpole stage within the egg. Gray's frog *Rana grayi,* of South Africa, lays its eggs in cup-shaped depressions in the ground but will also lay them in water. The larvae, on hatching, find their way to the nearest pool.

The dusky-throated frog *R. fuscigula* rivals the paradoxical frog in the size of its tadpole. The frog, which lives in mountain streams of East and South Africa, is 8 cm long. Its eggs, laid in shallow pools formed by hillside trickles in which the water is warm, give rise to larvae 4 cm long, while those laid in deeper water with lower temperatures give larvae up to 10 cm or even 17 cm long. In deep water they may remain in the tadpole stage for two or three years.

The hairy frog *Trichobatrachus robustus* of West Africa has fine glandular filaments along its flanks and thighs, and these look like hairs but are a form of gill. Only the male has them (presumably to offset the smallness of the lungs in this species) during the breeding season when he is the more active and aquatic and therefore in greater need of more oxygen. Another peculiarity is that the tips of the bones in three of the toes on each foot

the effect of an electric current. So the Ranidae, and the European species especially, take pride of place historically.

The European frogs known to Linnaeus were the common frog *Rana temporaria* and the edible frog *R. esculenta,* the hind legs of the latter having been long associated with the gustatory habits of the French. Both species can be called therefore the typical frogs, or true frogs. As the zoological frontiers of European scientists widened it was found that there were more striking frogs elsewhere in the world.

The most famous of all true frogs, thanks to Mark Twain, is the bullfrog *R. catesbeiana* of North America. It is up to 20 cm long and its call is said to resemble the lowing of cattle or the roaring of a bull. Some other large frogs in other parts of the world are also called bullfrogs.

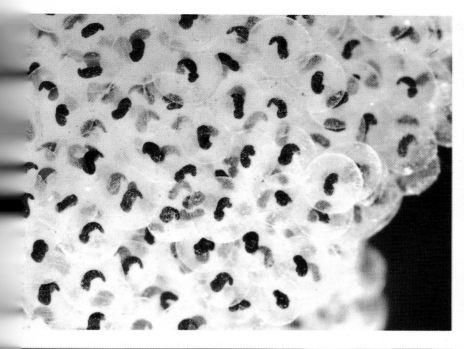

(Above) Wallace's flying frog, with its characteristic webbed feet which enable it to glide from tree to tree

(Far left) European common frogs in amplexus prior to spawning, beside a mass of spawn laid by another pair

(Top left) mass of spawn of European common frog in which embryos are developing

(Top right) globules from the spawn of the European common frog, showing the developing embryo at the centre

(Left) newly-hatched larvae of the European common frog hanging from the jelly-mass of spawn from which they have just emerged

are hooked so that the bones project beyond the skin. The function of this is unknown but recalls the condition in the dagger frog *Rana holsti*, of Okinawa. In the male there is a 'thumb' consisting of a long, pointed bone terminating in a spine which occasionally projects beyond the skin. Anyone handling the frog is liable to have this tip dug into his hand, drawing blood.

The family Hyperolidae is wholly African and contains the sedge frogs. They live on flying insects such as midges and mosquitoes in the sedge swamps. One of them, the arum frog, *Hyperolius horstocki*, is white and 2·5 cm long. It has the habit of sitting in an arum flower, where it is inconspicuous by reason of its colour, waiting for insects that visit the flower. When disturbed it can leap 60 cm away or 45 cm upwards, to cling to a leaf, stem or another flower. When the arum is no longer blooming the frog clings to stems with the expanded tips of its toes and changes colour to become brown with white stripes.

Wallace's flying frog of Malaya *Rhacophorus nigropalmatus* lives up in trees, leaping from branch to branch in search of flying insects. All four feet are strongly webbed. To move from one tree to another the flying frog jumps, spreads its legs for the webbed feet and flaps of skin on the arms and legs to act as parachutes, and pulls up its underside to form a concavity to buoy it still further. So it glides to another tree trunk perhaps 50 m away.

Several relatives of the flying frog make foam nests for their eggs among leaves or in a hole in the ground. As a pair are in amplexus and the eggs are being extruded the female beats up the jelly surrounding the eggs with her hind feet. The male clinging to her uses his hind feet to pull out the

(Right) reed frog Hyperolius viridiflavu of East Africa eating a damselfly. The frog looks somewhat like a tree frog (family Hylidae) but actually belongs to the family Hyperoliidae

(Left) edible frog of Europe which stays close to water into which it leaps at first alarm

(Left) frog of Microhylidae species, clinging to bamboo stem

(Below) female African tree frog Chiromantis xerampelina *(Rhacophoridae) beats the jelly of her spawn into a froth at her feet to make a protective nest for the developing embryos*

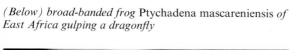
(Left) running frog Kassina senegalensis; *its call sounds like a cork popping*

(Below) broad-banded frog Ptychadena mascareniensis *of East Africa gulping a dragonfly*

strings of eggs from her body, at the same time fertilizing them.

The narrow-mouthed toads (Microhylidae) have bloated bodies and unusually small mouths. Their hind legs are not so long as those of typical frogs, which is why as a group they are called toads. Many of them live in shallow burrows in the ground, often far from water, in which case they lay their eggs under stones or in holes in the ground. The larvae remain within the egg membranes and hatch as froglets. Some narrow-mouthed toads feed almost entirely on termites,

even taking up residence in the termite nests, and the distribution of the Microhylidae as a whole is more or less the same as the distribution of termites – in a tropical belt around the world.

Continuing the confusion between the names 'frog' and 'toad', the rain frogs *Breviceps* are small and rotund, narrow-mouthed toads of southern Africa, with pug faces and short hind legs. They live in burrows in the ground, coming out in numbers when heavy rains occur. In addition to the toad-like appearance, rain frogs have many wart-like poison glands in the skin.

REPTILES
Tuataras, turtles, tortoises and terrapins

Reptiles being 'cold-blooded' animals are, like the amphibians, most numerous in the Tropics. However, it is a popular misconception that reptiles and amphibians are in fact cold-blooded. Unlike mammals and birds, they derive their heat from their surroundings by basking in the sun or on warm stones and some lizards even maintain a body temperature above that of a mammal. The outer skin of reptiles is covered by horny dead scales. It has no respiratory function but it plays an important role in conserving body fluids. Reptiles are also independent of water in their breeding so they are able to live in dry places. Fertilization is internal and the females lay large yolky eggs, with a leathery, or sometimes a hard, chalky shell. The other differences are in the internal anatomy and physiology.

Because they breathe through their skin a limit is set to the size amphibians attain. They are compelled to preserve a large surface area in proportion to their volume. The reason why some of the early amphibians, such as the labyrinthodonts, were large is probably that they were exclusively lung-breathing. Having no such restrictions reptiles were able to achieve tremendous size, to give rise to the largest land animals that ever lived, the brontosaurus and diplodocus.

The captorhinomorphs, of the Pennsylvanian period 300,000,000 years ago, were the most primitive of known reptiles. In their structure they closely resemble the terrestrial anthrocosaurian amphibians and reptiles have probably been derived from this labyrinthodont group.

By the Cretaceous period, from 135,000,000 to 70,000,000 years ago, the reptiles dominated the land surface. This period is called the Age of Reptiles, epitomized by the giant dinosaurs of up to 25 m in length (including the long slender neck and tail as in such giants as the diplodocus) and many tons in weight. It would be a mistake, however, to suppose that all the reptiles of this period were large. There were many more small and medium-sized reptiles than giants. Large and small, however, they dominated the land. They also dominated the air in the form of pterodactyls – the flying reptiles; and in rivers and seas, crocodiles and turtles, as well as the extinct plesiosaurs and ichthyosaurs, had no rivals.

It may not be amiss to refer at this point to the relish with which even informed people still persist in speaking of the ground trembling 'like a minor earthquake' as the giant reptiles of the past walked over it. Had they put their feet down with such force the jarring to their spine would have been intolerable!

At the close of the Cretaceous period the giant reptiles suddenly died out. There have been nearly as many theories put forward to account for this as there were species of giants then existing. None holds water except perhaps for the latest, that sunspots caused a sudden and catastrophic lowering of the earth's temperature. Whatever the cause may have been, there was a sudden elimination of many groups, especially of the large reptiles, and the elimination has meant that the reptile fauna of today is impoverished compared with that existing 70,000,000 years ago. Some groups persisted, however, notably the crocodiles, tortoises and turtles; and one group all but died out, leaving as sole survivor the tuatara of New Zealand, a celebrated living fossil.

The tuatara *Sphenodon punctatus* is the only remaining species of the order Rhynchocephalia, the remainder having become extinct 100,000,00

Tuatara, the lizard-like living fossil of New Zealand

years ago. Today the tuatara is found only on a few islands in Cook Strait and in the Bay of Plenty where it is strictly protected, but it was known to the Maoris on both North and South Island so it must have suffered a major eclipse within historical times.

The tuatara has remained virtually unchanged in structure for 130,000,000 years. It looks like a large lizard, up to 60 cm long, black-brown to dull green, sometimes with a reddish tinge. A crest of triangular folds of skin runs down the midline of the back and tail. In its skull and backbone it differs from true lizards.

Tuataras live in burrows which they can dig for themselves but on the islands where they now live they more often occupy the burrows made by petrels and shearwaters. Apparently these birds and the reptiles live harmoniously together although the tuatara sometimes eats their eggs and chicks. Its normal diet is insects and other small invertebrates, for which it forages at night.

An outstanding feature of the tuatara is its slowness in movement. It is able to withstand low temperatures and remains active at temperatures as low as 7°C. As a result it seldom hibernates. Its slowness is best epitomized by reports that it has been seen to fall asleep while chewing a mouthful of food. With a metabolism running at such a low

level it is not surprising to learn that it is long-lived. It grows very slowly and probably does not breed until 20 years old. It continues to grow in size until aged 50 or more and estimates of its life-span vary from 100 to 300 years.

Unlike all other reptiles the male lacks a copulatory organ, pairing being effected as in birds by the apposition of the cloacae of male and female. Pairing usually takes place in January, but conception is not until the following October to December, the sperm lying dormant within the female until then. This is a remarkably odd phenomenon and it is difficult to see what function can be served by it. When ready to lay the females scoop out a shallow nest in the soil in which they lay 5 to 15 soft-shelled white eggs. These do not hatch for a further 13 to 15 months.

The tuatara is famous also because it was in this species that the pineal eye, usually now called the parietal eye, was first fully investigated. This is sometimes referred to as a third eye or as the remains of a second pair of eyes in the top of the head. Many fossil skulls of reptiles show a hole in the top of the head. In tuatara there is a small eye beneath, about 5 mm in diameter, with a lens, a retina and an optic nerve. It can be clearly seen in the young tuatara but is covered with skin in the adult. Its function is problematic. It seems not to

45

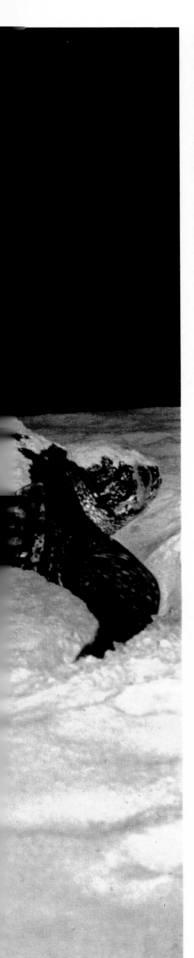

(Above) green turtle hatchling emerging from the egg. The egg has been artificially exposed for photographing

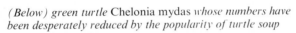

(Left) chiefly responsible for the decline in marine turtles are those who collect their eggs for food

(Below) green turtle Chelonia mydas *whose numbers have been desperately reduced by the popularity of turtle soup*

be sensitive to light, but remains of this 'pineal eye' are present in many amphibians and lizards and in a much modified form in other vertebrates, including man.

The Testudines, by which is meant turtles, tortoises and terrapins, would also qualify as living fossils, if there were not so many of them. A living fossil is an animal or plant that has outlived its era. The Rhynchocephalia were formerly wide-spread over the earth and all died out except the tuatara. The first Testudines appeared on the earth over 200,000,000 years ago and have remained relatively unchanged for the last 150,000,000 years. They are no less numerous than they used to be in the number of species, although their populations have been devastated almost everywhere by man.

The body of a turtle or tortoise is enclosed in a box or shell which is typically rigid and in most species the head, legs and tail can be withdrawn into it. In some species the outsides of the legs are covered with large plates, called scutes, partly horn, partly bone, giving added protection when the animal has withdrawn into its shell. The upper part of the shell, the carapace, is formed by a widening and thickening of the ribs, usually meeting to make a continuous roof of bone. The lower part, the plastron, is made up of bony plates. The whole shell is covered with scutes of horn. The sexes are alike but the males are usually smaller than the females and have a longer tail and a concave plastron.

The Testudines have no teeth; instead the jaws are covered with a horny beak. They are probably deaf, the ear being closed with a membrane, although it seems likely that they can pick up

(Above) tracks of a leathery turtle that has shuffled up the tropical beach to lay

(Above right) diamondback terrapin Malaclemys terrapin *which is famous as a delicacy at the table*

(Right) spotted turtle Clemmys guttata *of North America, a small freshwater turtle under 13 cm long*

vibrations through the ground. Their eyelids are moveable and are closed in sleep. All Testudines lay eggs, always on land, the marine and fresh-water turtles coming ashore to do so.

As a group, tortoises and turtles are noted for longevity although there are few reliable records of this. The best authenticated record is for Marion's tortoise *Geochelone gigantea,* known to have lived more than 152 years, but there are unconfirmed records of 200 years or more. A common garden tortoise, much smaller in size than Marion's tortoise, lived in the garden of Lambeth Palace, in London, for 120 years. Like the tuatara, tortoises probably owe their long life spans to never hurrying themselves.

The marine turtles live in warm seas. They are of seven kinds: the hawksbill, the green turtle, the flatback, the loggerhead, the two kinds of Ridley

turtle and the leathery turtle. The smallest is the hawksbill *Eretmochelys imbricata,* so named for its hooked beak. The scutes of its carapace overlap and are the source of tortoiseshell. The green turtle *Chelonia mydas* feeds mainly on the marine grass *Zostera* which may be why its fat is green; it is in demand for making turtle soup. Considerably larger than the hawksbill, it may reach 1·3 m in length. The loggerhead *Caretta caretta* is about the size of the green turtle and is of little value for its flesh or shell. Ridley turtles *Lepidochelys olivaceus* and *L. kempi* are the smallest sea turtles: their shells are round and reach no more than 70 cm in length. The leathery turtle *Dermochelys coriacea,* or luth, also called leatherback, is up to 3 m long and weighs nearly 2,000 kg. It feeds largely on jellyfishes. Its carapace is not joined to its ribs but is a mosaic of small bony plates covered with skin.

Marine turtles have the legs flattened to flippers, the shell is more flattened than in tortoises and except in Ridleys is shield-shaped in outline. They keep at sea except at the breeding season when the females come ashore on sandy beaches to lay. Each digs a deep hole well up the beach and lays about 100 eggs. She then fills the hole in and returns to the sea. Ten weeks later the tiny turtles dig their way to the surface and make their way to the sea. Turtle eggs have been collected on a large scale for food and this, added to adults killed for soup, and the large numbers of hatchlings that fall prey to sea-birds and predatory fishes, is why all turtles are becoming scarce.

Freshwater turtles are of two kinds: those which withdraw the neck in a vertical S-shape under the front part of the carapace (like sea turtles and land tortoises), and those which withdraw it sideways (side-necked turtles); the first group is much the more numerous.

The mud turtles and musk turtles of North

(Above) hinge shelle tortoise Kinixys bell *of tropical Africa is widespread and numerous in open country*

(Pages 50–51) snap turtle of the freshwa of North America

America are mainly small. They swim little but move slowly over the bottom of the shallow ponds, feeding on snails and other small invertebrates, fish, plants and carrion. In mud turtles the front and rear portions of the plastron are hinged and can be drawn up to enclose the soft parts of the animal. Musk turtles are so named for the strongly smelling excrement voided when they are disturbed and for this reason they are also known as stinkpots.

The American snapping turtles are widespread and numerous. They have strong hooked beaks. They seldom swim, but lie on the bottom in shallow waters, unable to withdraw the head but ready to snap at anything that disturbs them, capable of giving a severe bite with their strong beaks. The common snapper *Chelydra serpentina,* also known as the loggerhead snapper, is up to 38 cm long.

The big-headed turtle *Platysternon megacephalum,* of south-eastern Asia, the only species in the family Platysternidae, also has a downwardly hooked beak as well as an enormous head that cannot be withdrawn. It lives in mountain streams, feeding on molluscs.

The largest family is the Emydidae, or pond tortoises, of which there are 80 species. The European pond tortoise *Emys orbicularis* spends most of its time in water but occasionally comes out on land, mainly to bask in the sun. It extends to western Asia and also north-west Africa.

Pond tortoises are half-way between land tortoises and true freshwater turtles in shape and habits. They are mainly vegetarian, some wholly so while others may take animal food as well. Some of the pond tortoises of southern Asia have the lungs enclosed in bony boxes formed by the inner walls of the shell, presumably to protect the lungs from increased pressure when diving to the bottom of the deep lakes that form their normal habitat.

The European pond tortoise has its counterpart in North America in Blanding's turtle *E. blandingi,* which spends more time on land. There are also many other species in North America, including those known as scooters and sliders, and the species properly known as the diamondback terrapin, *Malaclemys terrapin.* The name 'terrapin' is from a Red Indian word meaning 'little turtle', which aptly describes it. The species has had a chequered history. In the 18th century it formed a cheap food for slaves. Then, as so often happens in foods and men's fashions, it found favour with the more fortunate. In the 19th century it became popular because its flesh was said to be more palatable than that of any other

Below) eastern box turtle, one of the most handsome turtles in the United States

53

turtle. Terrapin à la Maryland, a rich dish of terrapin flesh cooked with vegetables, wine and eggs, with sherry added before serving, became the vogue. As a result, the numbers of the terrapins dropped and legal protection was given to the species.

In the 20th century the keeping of 'terrapins' became popular and almost any small freshwater turtle was given the name. Chief among these are the red-eared terrapin *Pseudemys scripta*, the Spanish terrapin *Clemmys caspica*, and the geographic or map terrapin *Graptemys geographica*, of Missouri, the St. Lawrence river and the Great Lakes. The diamondback terrapin is so called for the bold sculpturing of the plates of the carapace, the red-eared has a red stripe along each side of the head and the map terrapin has markings on the carapace resembling a map. Fully grown, none of these exceeds 20 cm in length and those kept as pets are usually much smaller.

The spiny turtle *Geomyda spinosa,* is one of many species related to the 'terrapins' distributed over the Americas. In the young each marginal scute of the carapace is continued into a spine so that the edges of the carapace are saw-toothed. The spines grow less with age until they finally disappear. At the same time the turtle spends more and more time in water.

Confusion over the name 'terrapin' is made worse by the scientific name *Terrapene* having been given to the box turtles of North America, sometimes called box tortoises, the last name being justified because they look more like land tortoises with a high, domed carapace. Although good swimmers they spend most of their time on land. *T. carolina,* the Carolina box turtle, is the best known; it grows to 15 cm in length and its carapace is dark brown to black with yellow markings. Box turtles are so named for the way the shell can be closed. The plastron is hinged at the middle and the two halves can be pulled up so that the shell forms a closed box with the owner snugly inside.

Box turtles seem to be water turtles returning to life on land. The soft-shelled turtles, family Trionychidae, are by contrast markedly aquatic and some species go into brackish water or even the sea. They live in southern Asia, Africa and North America. Their carapace is not covered with horny scutes but with a thick leathery skin which projects well beyond the margin of the bony shield.

The second group of freshwater turtles are the side-necked turtles. They are found throughout the warm areas of the southern hemisphere.

(Right) Malayan soft shelled mud turtle Trionyx

(Below) western box turtle, common in the plains region of North America

One family, the Chelidae, includes the snake-necked turtles of Australia and South America. In some of these the neck is as long as the carapace.

Another member of this family is the well-known matamata *Chelys imbricata*, of South America. Its head is very flat and looks triangular because of the flaps of skin decorating it. The head terminates in front in a fleshy proboscis. The carapace also is decorated with flaps of skin effectively disguising its outline. So camouflaged, the brownish matamata is hard to see as it lies in wait on the bottom for a fish to pass near; then it opens its enormous jaws and the rush of water draws the fish well into the mouth.

More even than the aquatic Testudines and the marine and freshwater turtles, the land tortoises are proverbial for their slow movement, although some of the smaller kinds can at times move with surprising speed – surprising for a tortoise, that is. For this reason alone it is wiser to ignore the advice, sometimes given, that a garden tortoise needs only to be let loose in the garden. In less than a minute a pet tortoise can be beyond the boundary of a small backyard and out of sight, if it so chooses.

Not surprisingly, tortoises are mainly vegetarian. Some may eat small invertebrates at times, but the favourite food is fresh green seedlings, despite the old and deeply rooted idea that a garden tortoise is the gardener's friend because it feeds on slugs! Another favourite food of nearly all tortoises is animal excrement.

The 35 species of land tortoises live in a variety of habitats from dry regions to humid jungles in the warmer parts of the world, in all continents except Australia. This is why pet tortoises allowed

(Above) most remarkable of all freshwater turtles is the matamata

ages 58–9) giant
toise of Chatham
nd in the South
cific

some parts of the world, although this is implicit in the large numbers exported for sale as pets. It is even more dramatically demonstrated by observing the ground after a grass fire, in Greece for example, and noting the numbers of dead tortoises of all sizes, but mainly young ones, lying scattered in the ashes.

The largest tortoises are the giant tortoises of the Galapagos Islands, *Geochelone elephantopus*, and of Aldabra, *G. gigantea*. These may be up to 1·2 m long and weights of 227 kg are regularly exceeded – one weighed in 1847 was 409 kg. The smallest Testudines are rarely less than 15 cm long when fully grown. Among them are the spider tortoise *Pyxis arachnoides* of Madagascar and the mud terrapins of North America *Kinosternon*, with shell-lengths of 10 to 15 cm.

Giant tortoises grow quickly, at least in the early part of their long life. One from the Galapagos increased in weight from 12·7 to 166·2 kg in seven years. This is unusual, the normal gain per year being 6 to 13 kg until 115 kg is reached, when the rate of growth tapers off.

Galapago is Spanish for tortoise, and the first Spaniards to visit the group of islands in the Pacific, off the north-west coast of South America, were so impressed with the numbers of giant tortoises they saw that they called the islands Galapagos. The animals provided them with meat and hungry seafarers in the centuries that followed stopped at the islands to replenish their supplies of fresh meat. In the present century alarm has been felt that these giant links with the past might become entirely eliminated and steps have been taken to protect them.

Land tortoises are generally inoffensive. The only known instance of a man being killed by a tortoise occurred in Ancient Greece. The bald poet Aeschylus was sitting out of doors when a lammergeier flew overhead with a tortoise in its beak. The habit of the lammergeier, or bearded vulture, is to carry bones up high and drop them onto rocks to break them, in order to eat the marrow. This one may have mistaken the bald head for a rock – or more likely its aim was bad. At all events, the tortoise cracked Aeschylus' skull and killed him.

The best known of the land tortoises are the so-called garden tortoises. Since their appearance and way of life is very similar, attention will be given to the Iberian or Algerian tortoise, *Testudo graeca* and the Greek or Hermann's tortoise *T. hermanni*. Both are up to 30 cm long and both have high, domed shells. Their legs are covered with hard scutes, which often have bony cores, and the five toes on the forefeet and the four toes

indoors in temperate regions will, if allowed, rest near a fire or under a radiator.

Tortoises mate in spring, the act of mating often lasting several hours. Courtship is limited and seems to consist only of the male butting the female in the side with its head. Solitary garden tortoises demonstrate this when they persist in butting the foot of a person sitting in the garden, or butting the leg of the chair. Males sometimes fight, a slow-motion combat, in which each seeks to turn the other on its back, a position from which it has difficulty in righting itself. The females lay spherical eggs with a firm parchment shell; they dig a hole to deposit the eggs then cover them with earth, after which they wander away. There is no parental care.

One surprising aspect of tortoise biology is the numbers in which the smaller tortoises exist in

on the hind feet all have long claws. When the head and legs are completely withdrawn into the shell the scutes give protection. The front legs are pulled back to make the elbows meet in the middle, so protecting the front entrance; the hind legs and tail are withdrawn and the soles of the feet block the entrance at the back. A third European species *T. marginata* is found only in southern Greece and on the island of Sardinia. It was taken to Sardinia by soldiers during World War II.

In south-western and central Asia lives the four-toed tortoise *T. horsfieldi,* the only tortoise with four toes on the forefeet as well as the hind feet. It is also remarkable for being active for only three months of the year. It spends the remaining nine months dormant in a burrow in the ground.

In the New World, species of the genus *Testudo* are found in South America only. In North

60

America their place is taken by the gopher tortoises, in the desert regions of the southwest. The South American species include the wood tortoise *T. denticulata* and the coal tortoise *T. carbonaria* which feed exclusively on carrion.

The four species of gopher tortoises are named from the French *gaufre,* meaning a honeycomb. This is an allusion to their burrowing. *Gopherus polyphemus,* the gopher tortoise, exemplifies all four species. During the heat of the day gopher tortoises take shelter in their burrows in the ground. Each burrow is a long passage ending in a large chamber. They emerge at dusk, when the air temperature has dropped, to feed on cacti.

The flat tortoises *Homopus* of southern Africa have a flattened carapace. They dig for the roots of grasses which form their staple food. Another unusual tortoise is the flexible tortoise *Kimixys* of Africa. The rear part of its carapace is hinged and can be drawn down like the visor of a helmet. A third unusual type, also African, is Tornier's tortoise *Malacochersus tornieri* of East Africa. It has a very flat carapace and the bones of it have almost disappeared, leaving only the horny scutes. This tortoise can run fast and to escape danger it runs to shelter among rocks. It goes into the nearest opening then inflates itself so that it becomes firmly wedged and cannot be pulled out.

(Below) African spurred tortoise Geochelone sulcata *beneath a flowering acacia tree*

Crocodilians: crocodiles, alligators and caimans

The crocodiles, with their relatives the alligators and caimans, are another ancient race, escaping the title 'living fossil' for the same reason as that given for the Testudines. The earliest known fossils are from the Triassic rocks of 200,000,000 years ago.

They are characterized by having the body covered by horny scales overlying bony scutes especially along the back. These are large, approximately square and arranged more or less in longitudinal and transverse rows. The forelegs are short, the hind legs longer and all feet are webbed. The tail is long and powerful, primarily for swimming, but it can also be used for attack. The head is long, consisting mainly of long jaws armed with conical teeth set in sockets. The nostrils and eyes are set high on the head, so that the animal can almost completely submerge – to the point of being hidden from oblique view – yet still be able to see and breathe. The ear meanwhile is closed by a flap of skin to keep water out.

A crocodile, alligator or caiman feeds when very young mainly on insects but may take other small aquatic animals. Later it graduates to taking fish and frogs as well; and well-grown adults eat mammals and reptiles and occasionally birds. Reports from different areas of Africa show that small or medium-sized mammals, or birds, may be seized when they go to drink in a crocodile-infested lake or river. In some regions human beings are liable to attack with sufficient frequency that measures, such as erecting a palisade of posts, need to be taken in places where people go to draw water. Strangely, in other regions crocodile attacks on people are rare or unknown. The explanation for this has yet to be found.

Since these aquatic reptiles feed mainly – exclusively when young – underwater, an examination of the inside of the mouth is interesting. The internal nostrils open at the extreme rear of the palate, almost into the throat when necessary. So, even when the mouth is opened underwater, while the nostrils are exposed at the surface, the animal can still breathe. Moreover, the salivary glands are at the back of the mouth. Other features of the mouth are that the tongue is completely fastened to the floor of the mouth and that new teeth grow throughout life, pushing out and replacing the old ones.

Crocodiles are especially active at night. They see well, for the same reason that a cat has good night vision: behind the retina is a tapetum, or reflecting layer, and the light passing through the eye which would otherwise be lost, is reflected back, so the maximum use is made of such light as is available. Smell and hearing are also acute, and from the convolutions on the surface of the brain it is reasonable to suppose that crocodilians are relatively intelligent, when they are compared with other reptiles.

Between the scales on the upper back are glands the secretion from which keeps the scales supple. On the underside of the lower jaw are tubular sacs which in moments of stress are everted; their function is not known. In the region of the cloaca are musk glands which probably help the sexes to find each other. In the breeding season the bellowing of the males forms another means of communication between the sexes. Except in the Mississippi alligator and the gharial of the Ganges it is hardly possible to tell the sexes apart externally.

Gharial or gavial Gavialis gangeticus *which uses its slender snout to catch fishes with a sideways sweep of the head*

64

Fertilization is internal. Mating takes place in the water, after which the female lays on land 100 or more eggs with chalky shells. The nest may be a simple pit in the sand, covered in after the eggs are deposited, or it may consist of a heap of mud or decaying vegetation. After 8 to 10 weeks, the time varying with the species, the eggs hatch. Most crocodilians show a certain amount of parental care, the mother staying beside the nest and, being in an irritable mood, shows fight at any intruder, whatever its intentions. Even so, the eggs are often taken. In Africa the most notorious egg-raider is the Nile monitor.

The baby crocodiles call with a sort of quack while still in the egg, announcing the imminence of hatching. The hatchlings are 20 to 30 cm long, and after being assisted by the mother, who removes the overlaying material on hearing their

calls, leave the nest and follow her to the water. Their first days are fraught with hazards, mainly that of being devoured by the larger crocodiles. To counter this, the babies tend to keep apart from the larger crocodiles, usually in the shelter of an overhanging bank.

Crocodiles become sexually mature at 8 to 10 years and until then they grow in length at about 30 cm a year. After this the growth rate decreases considerably. Some species do not exceed 2 m in length when fully grown and most never exceed 3·5 m. The largest crocodile was once thought to have measured 8·2 m but recent examination of the skull (which is preserved in the Museum of Comparative Zoology at Harvard University) suggests that the specimen killed in 1854 at Jala Jala, on Luzon island of the Philippines, could not have been more than 7 m long. It belonged to the

species known as the salt-water or estuarine crocodile *Crocodylus porosus* distributed from northern Australia to the Philippines. The largest fossil crocodile so far unearthed was estimated to be 10 m long in life. The Nile crocodile *Crocodylus niloticus,* the species ranging over much of Africa, usually does not exceed 4 m but a reliable record gave a maximum of nearly 6 m.

The smallest crocodilian is the West African dwarf crocodile *Osteolaemus tetraspis,* which rarely exceeds 1 m length. The dwarf caiman *Paleosuchus palpebrosus* rarely reaches 1·2 m.

Crocodiles and alligators all look much alike. Examination of the teeth when the mouth is shut, however, gives an instant clue. In a crocodile the teeth in both upper and lower jaws are in line but in an alligator the upper teeth lie outside the lower when the mouth is shut. In an alligator the fourth tooth fits into a pit in the upper jaw. In a crocodile it fits into a notch in the upper jaw and can be seen even when the mouth is shut, giving a crocodile a perpetual toothy grin.

There are two species of alligator: the North American *Alligator mississipiensis* (the scientific name is spelt with only one 'p' because of a misspelling in the original description, and the internationally accepted rule is that the first published name must stand), and the much smaller (less than 2 m) Chinese alligator *A. sinensis.* The second of these was unknown to the western world until 1879. It lives in the Yangtse River.

South America has, in addition to other crocodilians, five species of caiman of three kinds: one

(Above left) eye of the spectacled caiman— note the narrowed pupil of an animal that uses its eyes mostly at night

species of black caiman *Melanosuchus,* two
species of smooth-fronted caimans, *Paleosuchus,*
and two of spectacled caimans, genus *Caiman.*
The last are so named for a ridge of bone con-
necting the eye-sockets and looking like the nose-
piece of a pair of spectacles. In general appearance
and in habits caimans do not differ much from
crocodiles and alligators, except for one important
difference. In all crocodilians the bony plates that
form an armour on the back occur under the
belly skin of caimans and so render the caiman
hide commercially worthless. This armour which
is a very definite feature after the flesh has
decayed, is an adaptation to life in swift rivers
with rocky banks and with boulders.

Crocodiles and alligators everywhere have
been threatened for some years by hunters
meeting the demand for their skins to make leather
for handbags and shoes. This has resulted in
making large crocodilians rare, the numbers of
crocodiles and alligators generally much smaller,
and causing alligators, especially in the United
States, to be given legal protection. But it has also
given a stimulus to crocodile-farming, with the
aim of releasing animals when past their infancy
in traditional habitats now denuded of crocodiles,
and possibly to satisfy the market demand for
crocodile hide as well.

(Top) leopard gecko Eublepharis macularis

(Above) palmate gecko, of the Namib desert, sloughing

(Right) flying gecko Ptychozoon *species of South-East Asia at rest. The fold of skin that helps the gecko to glide is lying along the side of its body*

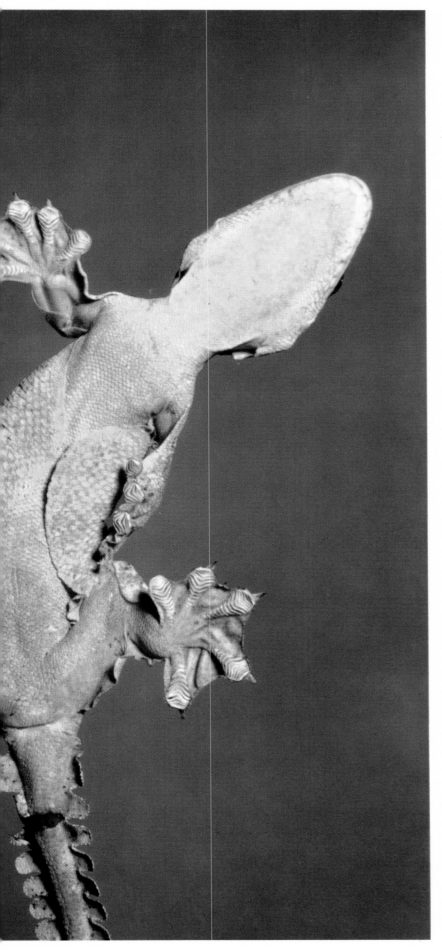

Lizards

The last division of the class Reptilia is the order Squamata which includes the lizards and snakes. Together they represent the most numerous reptiles today and the most modern. The lizards are the more primitive of the two. Generally, they have well-developed limbs, although in a small minority legs may be small or absent altogether. There are typically five toes on each foot with strong claws. The skin scales are often supported by bony plates and the belly scales are usually larger than those on the back and sides and are arranged in regular longitudinal rows. A well-known feature of some lizards is the ability to cast part of the tail when in danger, and to grow a replacement.

The most primitive of the lizards are the geckos, insect-eating reptiles distributed throughout the world's warmer latitudes, even on oceanic islands. There are nearly 700 species noted for their climbing abilities, nocturnal habits and for the use of their voice. Many have retractile claws, and most have friction pads on the toes enabling them to climb a vertical surface, even a pane of glass, and to walk upside down on a ceiling.

Geckos are found in forests, swamps and deserts, the desert forms having 'snowshoe' pads on which they can scamper swiftly across loose sand. They are also found on mountains and islands wherever the nights are not unduly cold.

The smallest geckos are 5 cm long and the largest 30 cm long, about half the total length being tail. All are covered with a soft skin with small scales and, in some species, a few larger scales. The feet, the chief distinguishing feature, usually have some of the scales on the underside of each toe forming broad pads furnished with hook-like bristles or bristles ending in minute suckers for clinging to smooth surfaces in the way already described. The peculiar wriggling gait of a gecko is due to these, since each time a foot is lifted the animal must curl each toe upwards from the front, to disengage the pads.

The eyes are usually large and often brightly coloured. The transparent lids in most geckos are permanently fused for protection. Dust or other foreign bodies settling on the eyes can be licked off with the long tongue. In those geckos that have movable lids the tongue is still used to lick the eyes. Because most geckos are nocturnal they cannot stand bright light, and so in daylight the iris in nocturnal forms is closed to a vertical slit the edges of which are scalloped allowing the animal to peer through a series of pin-holes.

(Left) East African gecko Hemidactylus species sloughing. Pa[rt] of the sloughed skin [is] still loosely attached

(Left) eye of a nocturnal East Africa[n] gecko Hemidactylus species showing the keyhole slit of the pu[pil]

(Right) common or green iguana Iguana iguana of tropical America, agile in the trees and speedy over the ground

The tail is important not only as a balancer but as a protection. Geckos that run slowly can throw off part of the tail to confuse a pursuer. In some species the tail resembles a caterpillar, which a pursuer presumably turns aside to consume, leaving the gecko to escape. In other species the tail is elaborately shaped and coloured to resemble a lichen or a leaf. A few species store reserve food, in the form of fat, in the tail. Geckos will also wave their tails like cats and some, when irritated, rattle the tail against the ground.

Some geckos are mute but most have calls, those of the females being different from those of the males. The call is often a tik-tik uttered several times in succession. In many other instances the calls are chirps, creaks and barks, and several species have received local names based on the sounds they make, like the cheechak *Hemidactylus frenatus* and the tokay *Gekko gecko*. Correlated with the use of the voice their hearing is acute.

Geckos lay two eggs (smaller species lay only one) and these may be laid under bark, in damp ground or merely glued to a vertical surface. A gecko 150 mm long will lay eggs over 12 mm in diameter. The hatchling is about half the size of its parent and from then growth is rapid, sexual maturity being reached by the age of one year, or two years at the most.

The family of lizards most nearly related to the geckos are the snake lizards (family Pygopodidae) of Australasia with two species in New Guinea and a dozen in Australia. The largest is 60 cm long. They are all snake-like but have the fleshy tongue of a gecko and use it to clean the eye. They can cast their tails in moments of danger and in certain features of their internal anatomy they show a close relationship to geckos. In all species the forelegs have been entirely lost and the hind legs are of little use being no more than flaps of skin with a miniature set of limb bones inside; these flaps being normally held flat to the body. Snake lizards progress over the ground with a serpentine movement of the body and tail.

The largest family of lizards and the one most reminiscent of reptiles of the past, at least in appearance, is the Iguanidae, the iguanas. They are restricted to the New World except for a few in Madagascar and Polynesia. Iguanas range from 13 cm to 2 m long. Some are insectivorous, others carnivorous, herbivorous or omnivorous (eating both plant and animal). The family also contains one species that gets its living from the sea, *Amblyrhynchus cristatus,* of the Galapagos Islands. It lives on the rocks in large numbers entering the sea to feed on seaweed.

The common or green iguana *Iguana iguana,* of Central and northern South America and, by

*(Left) rhinoceros
iguana* Cyclura cornuta
*of Haiti. It gets its
name from the
horn-like scales on its
nose*

*(Below left) the green
or common iguana can
alter its shades of
green*

*(Below) close-up of the
eye of the common or
green iguana*

introduction, some of the Caribbean islands, is 2 m long, green, and with a crest like the teeth of a comb running down the centre of the back and tail. Males are larger than the females, their crests stand higher and they have more orange or yellow colouring.

Green iguanas are agile tree-climbers and speedy over the ground. Their agility is best expressed by the way one of them will fall from a tree to the ground 13 to 18 m below and, with hardly a pause, sprint for the nearest undergrowth. Often they frequent trees overhanging water into which they will drop to escape, swimming underwater, propelled by the tail, and surfacing under cover of overhanging vegetation. Their reflexes are rapid and they are hard to hold as they struggle, biting and scratching. The common iguana has a row of saw-edged scales on the tail which can be whipped at a predator. A boa

constrictor or a hawk may take an iguana, but the iguana's worst enemies are man and his domestic animals. At sight of a hawk an iguana 'freezes' and local hunters use this to catch the lizard, imitating the cry of a hawk and seizing the iguana while it is immobile.

Green iguanas eat insects when young but feed as adults on young shoots, flowers, leaves and fruits. Ground iguanas can climb trees but spend most of their time feeding on vegetation and small animal life on the ground. One of the largest is the rhinoceros iguana *Cyclura cornuta* of Haiti. It is the heaviest but not the longest. It has heavier jaws than most others and a grotesque pattern of enlarged scales on the head three of which, on the snout, are pointed and look like horns.

Iguanas are generally either solitary or they live in pairs, the males being highly territorial. The crest along the back is supplemented by a throat

(Above) this anole lizard kept as a pet continually displayed aggressively at his own reflection and even tried to bite it

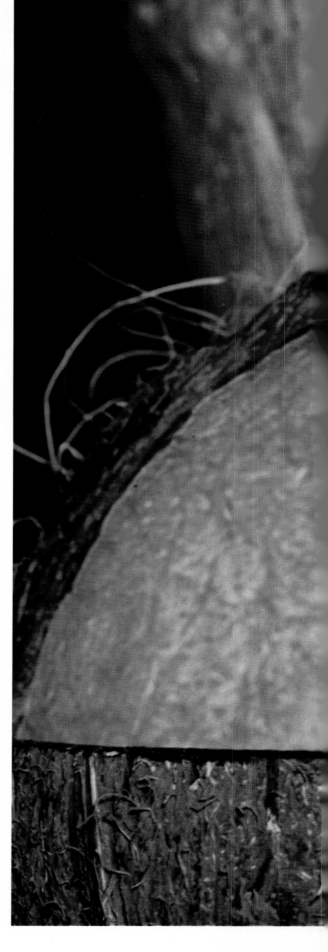

fan which can be inflated to intimidate a rival. Iguanas use no voice but sometimes they emit gurgling hisses when cornered.

Also in the Iguanidae are the anoles, American lizards of which there are 165 species, the best known being the green anole *Anolis carolinensis*. Anoles are also known in America as chameleons for their ability to change colour rapidly. They are highly territorial, and the males display at each other, especially by inflating a reddish throat sac.

Anoles, which range from 12 to 48 cm in length, are continually on the move in the daytime, searching for insects in bushes and trees or on the ground. Their toes bear small sharp claws and have adhesive pads with minute transverse ridges enabling them to cling to smooth surfaces.

Two remarkable lizards also belong to this family: one is the basilisk, and the other is the horned toad. The several species of basilisk range from Central America to central Mexico, frequenting the banks of small rivers. They are slender lizards, mainly green in colour and with long slender toes, the males often adorned with a high crest. They feed by day on insects, small rodents and birds and sleep by night on bushes overhanging the water.

When alarmed a basilisk makes for the water, usually dropping onto it from a bush. It may sink

(Right) American anole lizards mating

immediately or it may scutter across supported by fringes of scales on the toes of the hind feet. As its speed slackens it slowly sinks and must then swim or dive and come up farther on. One local name for the basilisk is tetetereche, in imitation of the sound it makes when scuttering. Another is the Jesus Cristo lizard, from its ability to run across water on its hind legs. A basilisk's foot is similar to that of a frog, with a broad sole to assist scuttering. There is an East-Indian water lizard and at least one species of frog capable of scuttering over water.

The largest and most colourful basilisk, with ornamented crests on the head, the back and the tail, is the green-crested basilisk *Basiliscus plumbifrons* of Costa Rica. It is up to 60 cm long.

The basilisk of mythology, after which the lizard is named, was supposed to be the King of the Serpents, so deadly that its glance alone was fatal to man and beast. There is nothing like this quality in its modern namesake. The only thing they have in common is the crest.

The horned toad looks also like something out of mythology and, like the modern basilisk, is equally harmless. It is a lizard and should more properly be called the horned lizard. There are a dozen species in the dry areas from Nebraska to Chihuahua and Sonora in Mexico. The horned toad, if it were larger, could pass for a prehistoric monster. It is only 12·5 cm long at most, with a squat, flattened and almost circular body, short legs and a short tail. The head is ornamented with long, backwardly-directed spines and most of the rest of the body is decorated with short spines; a typical species is *Phrynosoma coronatum*. Some of the species have short spines round the back of the

(Right) one of the spiny-tailed lizards (Uromastyx) living in the desert of south-eas Morocco

(Below right) eastern collard lizard Crotaphytus collaris, *noted for the rich variety of its colours and patterns*

(Below) modern basili noted not for its virule qualities but for its ability to run across tl surface of water

head, a less pronounced corona, and are called short-horned.

Horned toads live in deserts and semi-deserts, at up to 3,000 m altitude. They hunt insects, particularly ants, and drink dew, taking both with the tongue which is shot out and withdrawn in a flash. As the day draws to a close a horned toad will sink into the warm sand, pushing its blunt head into the sand and wriggling its body until immersed. Its mottled colouring of browns and greys is an effective camouflage, while its numerous spines tend to deter its few enemies. The snake that samples one is likely to succumb from the longer of these spines piercing its gullet.

It is the more astonishing, therefore, to note the horned toad's curious mechanism for squirting blood from the eyes. It has been suggested that this is defensive, that the blood is an irritant to the eyes of smaller mammals, but the habit is strangely erratic. A hundred horned toads may be handled without witnessing it or the first one picked up may give a demonstration of it. So far there has been no fully satisfactory explanation of this habit.

Another large family of lizards is the Agamidae. It differs from most other lizards in having teeth fixed by their bases on the ridge of the jaw. Also, the tongue is short, thick and slightly forked. The

300 species, small to medium-sized and none larger than 1 m long, the majority being much smaller, are distributed over the Old World tropics, few reaching temperate latitudes. One of these is the hardun *Agama stellio* of the southern Balkans. A few others live in Central Asia.

Agamids live on the ground, among rock or in trees. The best known is the common agama *Agama agama* of Africa, 30 cm long. The male is dark blue except for the terracotta head. Its skin is rough to the touch and the legs are long, the toes bearing strong claws. During the day agamas hunt insects, but they also eat grass, seeds, berries and eggs of other lizards. At night they roost communally, the males going dull brown like females.

Agamas are the most common reptiles of West

(Far left) blue-throated agama of Kenya in aggressive display, holding its head back to expose the coloured throat

(Left) Indian bloodsucker Calotes versicolor, *an agamid lizard which receives its name from the red colour which the male sometimes assumes. It does not suck blood*

Africa. They are everywhere in bush and forest, in the villages, running up and down walls of houses even in the towns. They may be all sizes from 12 to 30 cm and coloured sandy or chocolate, with green-spotted heads or orange blotches on the flanks. In fact, they show so many colour patterns that there would seem to be an infinity of species.

The common agama is polygamous, a brightly-coloured male occupying a territory with a dozen or more females, vigorously driving away intruders. Fighting is common between the males, who bob their heads up and down threateningly, then lash out with their tails or snap at each other with their jaws.

Other members of the Agamidae include the toad-headed agamids, the spiny-tailed lizards, the Australian moloch or thorny devil, the bearded lizard, the frilled lizard and the flying dragons.

The toad-headed lizards *Phrynocephalus* are small, up to 20 cm long, with disproportionately large heads and wide mouths. They live in the deserts and semi-deserts of Central and West Africa. Their colours match their surroundings, and for further protection they have the ability to bury themselves rapidly in the sand.

The spiny-tailed lizards *Uromastyx* are among the few burrowing agamids. They live in the deserts of North Africa and south-western Asia. They feed on flowers, leaves and fruits and will also eat dried plants. Their burrows may be as large as 3 m long by 1·5 m deep.

Moloch was a Canaanite god to whom children were sacrificed. It was a little unfair to pin the name on a harmless lizard belonging to the Agamidae. Yet this is what has happened to the thorny devil or moloch *Moloch horridus,* of Australia, 20 cm long, coloured orange and brown, and covered all over with spines. It feeds almost exclusively on ants, in deserts and semi-deserts. The moloch will position itself near a trail of ants and pick them off one by one, eating up to 5,000 in one session. The female moloch digs a hole in the sand in which to lay her ten eggs. Each egg is 25 mm long and 12 mm in diameter – an enormous egg for so small a lizard.

Australia is the home also of another lizard that looks like an antediluvian monster. It is the bearded lizard or bearded dragon *Amphibolurus barbatus.* Up to 60 cm long, grey to yellow, its whole body is beset with small spines. Around the snout, forming a sort of shield, is a throat pouch,

Its fierce appearance gave the moloch Moloch horridus *of Australia the name of mountain devil, but its spines hide the fact that it is a harmless agamid*

When alarmed the Australian frilled lizard raises its frill like an umbrella to deter an attacker

and when inflated the spines covering it stand out, looking like a beard. This beard is most conspicuous in courtship or when the lizard is facing a rival or an intruder. In courtship the male blows out his throat pouch to the fullest extent and opens his mouth to show the bright yellow lining to the female. He does the same to a rival male, or an intruder, but in addition raises his ribs making his body look bigger. The bearded lizard inhabits mostly scrub and desert country and the coast, especially of eastern Australia. It eats insects, small lizards, snakes and flowers.

Another Australian dragon, even more startling in appearance, is the frilled lizard *Chlamydosaurus kingii*. Up to 1 m long, it has a slender body, a long slender tail, and is a pale brown, usually with yellow and dark brown blotches. Its most conspicuous feature is a frill around the throat, which when not in use lies folded over the shoulders like a cape. It is a large fold of skin stiffened by rods of gristle that spring from the tongue bone and act like the ribs of an umbrella. When the lizard is excited from any cause such as fear, or when it is aggressive, it swings the frill forward – like a woman opening a parasol against a herd of inquisitive cows. The effect is the same. It is probably a scare device, and an effective one since when fully expanded the frill is as wide as the total length of the lizard's head and body. At the same time as the frill is expanded the lizard opens wide its enormous coloured mouth. If this warning display is disregarded the lizard walks towards the intruder, hissing. Even a dog has been known to retreat before this bold display.

Continuing with the story of the agamid dragons, most of the flying dragons or lizards feed exclusively on ants. There are a dozen species in the forests of India and south-eastern Asia, none of which is more than 30 cm long. There are other lizards that can parachute to the ground but only the flying lizards can control the angle of descent. The commonest is *Draco volans*, with blue wattles and dewlap. Its limbs are free for climbing along branches, but along each side of the flattened body is a thin skin stretched across movable and much elongated ribs. This is folded against the body except when the lizard takes to the air, then it is opened like a fan as the lizard launches itself into space. Then the lizard faces downwards, goes into a steep dive, straightens out at an angle of 22° and glides towards a neighbouring tree trunk. When about to land it banks, to land head uppermost.

Hardly less bizarre than the three 'dragons' of Australia and the Far East are the 90 species of chameleons (family Chamaeleonidae) which are found mainly in Africa and Madagascar. The

common chameleon *Chamaeleo chamaeleon* ranges through North Africa to Spain, Portugal and Malta and through the north of the Arabian peninsula to India and Ceylon. The smallest chameleons are hardly over 3 cm long, the largest 80 cm. All have the same specialized features.

The body is flattened from side to side and the head is often decorated with folds of skin, a crest or 'horns'. The eyes are set like turrets in the sides of the head with the eyelids grown together, leaving only a circle for the pupil. Many fishes, reptiles and birds can move the eyes independently to some degree, but in chameleons this independent movement is more pronounced. At any moment one eye may be looking forward, the other backward, keeping watch for insects.

Against enemies a chameleon has little defence other than its colour and general immobility,

such movements as it does make being in very slow motion. Chameleons are able to assume the colours of their background and, since they live in trees and shrubs, are usually seen as some shade of green or brown with various spots and other markings. If a part of the body is shaded by a leaf it goes pale yellow to white. When the chameleon moves into full light the light patch slowly returns to normal colour. At night most chameleons go pale.

Stories based on a chameleon's ability to make rapid and remarkable colour changes are exaggerated. They can adapt to some extent to the background colour; the more extreme changes are sometimes due to variation in the intensity of the light and in temperature, but they result more especially from changes in the animal's mood.

The two most remarkable features are the feet

and the tongue. The five toes on each foot are united into opposing bundles. On the front feet there are three toes on the inside, two on the outside, and on the hind feet this is reversed. Each foot is a pair of clasping tongs at the end of a long slender leg, capable of taking a very firm grip on a perch, aided by the prehensile tail.

The tongue can be shot out to a distance of almost half the lizard's total length, so the chameleon need do no more than wait for a flying insect to settle within striking distance. It has no need of speed or excessive movement. The essential part of the tongue is the tongue bone. When not in use the tongue is drawn back over this bone. When action is needed, the longitudinal muscles holding the tongue back are relaxed and the circular muscles are contracted. The tongue is shot out like an orange pip being squeezed between thumb and forefinger. The clubbed end is sticky, and high speed photography has also shown it can to some extent be used to grasp small prey. The shooting out of the tongue and its withdrawal are very rapid.

Despite the general calm of a chameleon's life territorial fighting sometimes takes place, mainly between males, but usually only as the result of restricted space in captivity. Such fights do show, however, that chameleons can bite and bite hard, inflicting serious – even fatal – injuries on each other. In the wild, to threaten is as a rule sufficient: two chameleons face each other at a distance, swaying slightly, the inflated body making any coloured patches more conspicuous, and the mouth often opening to display the coloured lining. The defeated opponent will change to an inconspicuous colour to acknowledge his submission.

Most chameleons lay eggs in holes in the ground, the female having to descend from her perch to dig these. A few species are ovoviviparous, as is the case in many reptiles, especially lizards and snakes. That is, the egg hatches as it is about to be laid, the baby inside rupturing the shell-membrane. The baby is therefore born alive and the female in such a case has no need to descend to the ground.

The next family of lizards is the skinks (Scincidae), with 600 species distributed over every continent apart from Antarctica. They are especially abundant in Africa, south-eastern Asia and the East Indian Archipelago and Australia. Skinks usually have cylindrical bodies, conical

Chameleon photographed in the act of catching a fly

heads, tapering tails and either short legs or none at all. Their scales are smooth so that typically a skink has a sleek, streamlined, almost metallic appearance. In many the eye is degenerate and covered by a scaly lower lid or by a transparent disk. No skink is truly aquatic, nor do they really run at any time. They crawl or at most scamper, thus conforming as a family to the original meaning of the name reptile, from the Latin *reptare,* to creep or crawl. They are secretive and many spend much of their time underground. The smallest are barely 7 cm long, and the majority are less than 20 cm long. The largest, the giant arboreal skink *Corucia zebrata* of the Solomon Islands is only 61 cm long; it is vegetarian.

Skinks feed mainly on insects except for the larger species the diet of which may be both insects and plant food or even wholly vegetarian. They are inoffensive, relying mainly on their retiring habits and on sacrificing their tails. A skink when threatened raises its tail in the air, turns it towards its attacker, waves it slowly back and forth and finally throws off half of it to wriggle violently or bounce about over the ground, so catching the attention of a would-be enemy, while the animal itself slips unobtrusively away. Some months later the tail is regrown to its original length, with simpler scales and a slightly different colour pattern. Not infrequently the tail will not be completely severed, in which event up to four extra tails may grow out from the broken surface.

These unobtrusive reptiles almost advertise the meekness which has allowed them to inherit the earth (as epitomized in their wide distribution) by their usually inconspicuous colouring. This is mainly brown or olive relieved in some species by spots, stripes and bars, and in a few

Profile of a male Jackson's chameleon Chamaeleo jacksoni *looking like a miniature prehistoric monster*

(above) close-up of the
front feet of the three-
horned or Jackson's
chameleon, showing how
the toes divide

(pages 92–3) new-born
babies of a viviparous
(live-birth) chameleon.
They can catch small
insects from birth

species by bright colours on the males at courting time. Their modesty conceals the fact that some skinks, contrary to what usually obtains in reptiles, make good parents. About half the species lay eggs, in clutches of 2 to 33, and the rest bear live young. Some American skinks tend their eggs until they hatch, one species brooding the hatchlings for a while.

There are, however, two species that have claimed notice, and both are Australian. One is the blue-tongued skink *Tiliqua scincoides,* up to 40 cm in length and so named for its blue tongue that it constantly flicks in and out. The other is the shingle-back lizard *Trachysaurus rugosus,* up to 45 cm long, also known as bobtail, boggi, double-headed lizard, pine-cone lizard and stumpy-tail, the multiplicity of names being sufficient indication that it has not passed un-noticed. The shingle-back is unusual in having

only two live young at a time, rarely triplets.

Another family, the Dibbanidae, may be related to skinks but there are strong reasons for believing they are more closely related to the geckos. They are blind, earless, burrowing lizards, living from south-eastern Asia to the Philippines, and in eastern Mexico. They live in or under rotting logs, feeding mainly on termites and one species is known from less than half a dozen specimens. Perhaps it is their rarity and obscurity that makes them the centre of super-stitions, as in Africa, where one species is supposed to be able to enter the human body at will. Its host, so the legend goes, will die when the lizard leaves his body. Other small burrowing lizards are *Feylinia* which although placed in the family Scincidae may justify later separation on account of differences in their skeleton.

In the grasslands of sub-Saharan Africa live

the girdle-tailed lizards or plated lizards (family Cordylidae). They are generally flattened horizontally, which enables them to slip easily into crevices among rocks for safety. The largest, the sungazer *Cordylus giganteus* is up to 37 cm long. All have a triangular head, covered with large scales (so gaining the name plated lizards), well-developed legs and a clubbed tail covered with whorls of large, keeled scales. In many species the neck and shoulders have folds of skin covered with more spiny scales. These spines are more than mere adornment and the ways in which they are used for protection are varied and ingenious. The commonest method is shown when the lizard is cornered, especially by snakes, and swings its tail vigorously from side-to-side, usually with good effect. One puff adder was seen to seize a girdle-tail and start swallowing it head-first. The tail was free to lash the snake's head, to such purpose that the adder released the lizard.

More commonly, passive methods are used. The lizard bolts into a crevice in the rocks and a would-be predator not only finds the entrance barred by the spines but is unable to extract the lizard because the spines are digging into the sides of the crevice. The lizard's spines around the neck and shoulders afford additional grip.

The armadillo lizard *Cordylus cataphractus*, 25 cm long, when intercepted and unable to reach a rocky refuge, rolls on its back and holds the end of its spiny tail in its mouth, so protecting the vulnerable belly. The sungazer already mentioned lies flat on the ground, its legs pressed to its sides and resists attempts to turn it over to attack the soft under-belly.

Included in the Cordylidae are four species of snake lizards which are long, slender and as their name suggests snake-like. Only one has the usual legs with four toes, the others have degenerate legs with only two toes on each leg and one of them has no front legs at all. A series like this illustrates the way limbs can be lost in the course of evolution to produce a snake-like reptile, such as the slow-worm.

The theme is continued in a group of plated lizards in southern Africa. In their internal anatomy these are intermediate between the skinks and the lacerta lizards, so suggesting another evolutionary link. In addition a number of them known as the whip lizards show yet another series in limb degeneration. One species has the usual five toes to each leg, another has four, a third has three toes on each foreleg and two on each hind leg, a fourth has one toe on each leg and a fifth has no front legs at all.

A totally different picture is presented by the wholly American family Teiidae, the members

of which are so diverse that nobody has attempted a common name to describe them. They are simply referred to as teiid lizards, largely confined to tropical America. The 200 or so species are of all types. Some have small scales, some have large scales. Most have well developed legs, others have tiny legs, reduced almost to vanishing point. Teiids show a great range of variation in their teeth. The front teeth are always conical, the usual lizard type, but those at the side may be conical, they may have two or three cusps, or they may be flat and molar-like teeth or large and broad crushing teeth.

Teiids are mainly carnivorous, including lizards, birds, mice, dead flesh and insects in their diet, but some also take fruit, others eggs. Species with crushing teeth live on snails. Most teiids are ground-living or burrowing, some live

in bushes and trees, and the caiman lizard *Dracaena guianensis,* with large scales like a caiman, is semi-aquatic and 1·2 m long. All, so far as is known, lay eggs.

Although there is no common name for the family it is rich in common names for the species. Among the larger teiids are the tegus which resemble the monitor lizards of the Old World. One tegu *Tupinambis nigropunctatus,* because of its fondness for eggs and chicks, is known as the poultry thief. The ameivas resemble the true lizards of Europe. Other teiids are the race runners, jungle runners and whiptails. In appearance most of the teiids could be mistaken for lacerta lizards, but they differ from them in details of their internal anatomy.

The lacerta lizards (Lacertidae) are found only in the Old World. They are taken to typify

lizards as a whole, but that is probably because study of lizards started in Europe. Nevertheless, it so happens this is a good choice of typical lizards. Most of the 150 species of Lacertidae have cylindrical bodies with a conical head and blunt snout covered with large scales. Small hexagonal scales cover the back and larger scales the flanks. The legs are well developed, and each bears five toes. The tail is long, tapering and covered with rows of oblong scales. The lower eyelid is freely movable and covered with very small scales. At each side of the head is an opening leading into the inner ear. The lacerta lizard's trick of casting off part of the tail and growing a new one is well known and we describe this in detail here for the common or viviparous lizard *Lacerta vivipara* of Europe.

In trying to capture this agile lizard 16 cm total length, of which 10 cm is tail, care must be exercised. Otherwise the catcher, having taken the lizard in his hand, finds himself with an empty hand, a few blood spots on the palm, and nothing else. On the ground the other half of the long tail, with its bloody end will be seen bouncing and bounding like an animal acting under its own volition. As likely as not the catcher's atten-

tion will have been caught by this extraordinary spectacle and he will have failed to notice the rest of the lizard drop to the ground and quietly disappear into the grass. In time it will grow a new tail, but not as perfect as the part it jettisoned to save its life.

This can happen even though the catcher does not take hold of the tail. Apparently the casting away of the tail is under nervous control, and takes place at a defined line of weakness or breaking point. At that point one of the vertebrae is naturally almost in two halves and requires only slight pressure to break it. The main blood vessels narrow at this point so that they can be severed with a minimum loss of blood. The main nerves also narrow at this point. In short, from early life if not from infancy onwards, the tail is prepared by its inherent structure for being severed with the least trauma for the animal. The idea that in sacrificing its tail the lizard diverts the attention of a potential predator seems eminently reasonable. Certainly that is what happens with the human observer.

The night lizards (family Xantusiidae) are exclusively American and resemble lacerta lizards except in habits. They live in the western United

(Above) green lizard Lacerta viridis, *and below it a wall lizard,* Lacerta muralis. *They are both of Europe, the first being up to 50 cm long*

States through Mexico to Central America, with one species in Cuba. Most of them spend the day in rock crevices, especially in flaking rock, one species living in rotting logs of yucca. They come out at night to hunt insects.

The slow-worm *Anguis fragilis* (family Anguidae) is a legless lizard with smooth scales, up to 50 cm long. It is olive-grey to bronze and the males are often blue on the back. The young are silver to golden with a black line along the back. Slow-worms are found over temperate Europe, south-western Asia and North Africa, where they are often killed by people who are under the impression that slow-worms are snakes. They feed on insects, slugs and earthworms and spend much of the summer season buried just under the ground, coming out at night to feed. At the other side of the world, in California, there are two

species of legless lizards (family Anniellidae) related to and differing in relatively small details from the slow-worms.

In spite of the frightening appearance of some lizards and of beliefs in the venomous nature of some of them that appear in folklore, there are only two species of poisonous lizards. Both live in North America. One is the Mexican beaded lizard *Heloderma horridum*, the other is the Gila monster *H. suspectum*, both of Mexico and the southwest United States. They range up to 80 cm and 50 cm long respectively. The Gila monster is black or dark-brown mottled with pink or yellowish-white. The beaded lizard is more black. Both have grooved teeth in the front of the jaws and when they seize their prey, such as nestling birds and the babies of small mammals, and start to chew, venom runs down the grooves and into

(Below) male green lizards fighting, trying to seize each other by the jaw in what can only be described as a trial of strength

Glass snake Ophisaurus apodus *of southern Europe. This is a legless lizard which sometimes displays minute hind limbs*

the victim's wounds, immobilizing it. They are stocky reptiles with a thick, short tail.

For real monsters among lizards it is necessary to turn to the monitors (family Varanidae). The smallest of these is the short-tailed monitor *Varanus brevicauda,* 20 cm long, of Australia. The largest is the Komodo dragon *V. komodoensis,* up to 3 m or more long, living on the small island of Komodo and a few adjacent islands in the East Indian Archipelago. A typical monitor has a heavy body, long neck and head, and a long, thick tail. The legs are strong with five toes on each foot, each toe bearing long, curved claws. Some of the details of the skeleton of a monitor, together with the possession of a forked tongue, have suggested a relationship with snakes; opinion has now veered from the idea, but they could be related to snakes' ancestors.

Monitors are unusual among lizards for being able to swallow large prey. The bones of their jaws are movable on each other, allowing a wide gape, and their teeth are long, curved, and serrated on the rear edge so they can seize prey and, in some species, tear it to pieces. The forked tongue is used, as in snakes, in conjunction with Jacobson's organ (the organ of chemical sense) in the roof of the mouth so that monitors can track their prey by the scent trail it leaves behind.

Monitors are distributed over the countries bordering the Indian Ocean, from Africa to Australia, some living in deserts. The Nile monitor *V. niloticus* readily takes to water and is said to ravage the nests of crocodiles and it also takes to stealing chickens. The monitors of southern and south-eastern Asia live in trees, either using hollow trees for shelter or climbing among the branches, although most rest in burrows, usually those excavated by other animals. The Australian monitors are known as goannas, said to be a corruption of iguana, from a supposed resemblance to those lizards.

The Komodo dragon, the largest of living

(Above) exceptional among lizards are the Mexican heloderm shown here and its relative the Gila monster, both of which use a venom on their prey

reptiles, was unknown outside its native home before 1912. It feeds on carrion and also kills such mammals as pigs, deer and monkeys, eating heavy meals that last for days.

Another recent discovery in the same area as the Komodo dragon is the earless monitor *Lanthanotus borneensis* (family Lanthanotidae). It was first discovered in Sarawak, in 1878, and little more was seen of it until 1960. It is up to 46 cm long, of an earthy brown colour, with very short legs. It moves in a semi-serpentine manner, pushing with its feet, and is active mainly at night. Earless monitors lie motionless in still water, such as in the irrigation ditches of rice fields, in wet soil or in burrows, pushing their noses out from time to time to take a breath. They resemble snakes in many ways even to hissing when being handled, and they give some indication what the ancestors of snakes may have looked like and how they behaved.

(Above) Burton's snake lizard Lialis burtoni, *one of the flap-footed lizards of Australasia, eating a gecko*

(Right) a monitor lizard with a typically heavy body, long neck and head

Slow worm Anguis fragilis, *a completely legless lizard
frequently mistaken for a venomous snake and killed*

Snakes

(*Below*) *best known of all the snakes that kill by asphyxiating their prey is the boa constrictor*

(*Bottom*) *emerald tree boa* Boa canina *which lives in the tree-tops and feeds on birds*

There is little in the fossil record to show how snakes originated. The general assumption is that they came from a lizard-like ancestor that took to a burrowing habit. The earliest snake fossil known is a 2 m, boa-like creature from the Cretaceous of Argentine and is about 100,000,000 years old, but the main development, and certainly the diversification of modern snakes, began about 20,000,000 years ago.

Snakes are elongated, legless reptiles. Some lizards are also elongated and legless, but whereas in all legless lizards there are still traces of the shoulder bones, these are entirely lacking in snakes. Only a few snakes have traces of hind legs or pelvis and these are not used in locomotion.

Snakes have no movable eyelids or ear-drum. They are usually said to be deaf and able only to pick up vibrations through the ground, but recent researches have shown they can pick up

103

airborne vibrations but only those from the middle C to the high C. Another characteristic feature of snakes is the forked tongue which is constantly flicked in and out when they are active, to test the surroundings. When the tongue is withdrawn into the mouth, the two tips of the forks are inserted into twin pits in the roof of the mouth, the Jacobson's organ, the organ of chemical sense. Presumably molecules picked up by the tongue tips are passed to it for sampling.

All snakes have a wide gape. This is possible because the two halves of both upper and lower jaws work independently of each other. The wide gape makes possible the swallowing of prey larger in diameter than the snake's body, and this is swallowed whole. The two halves of both upper and lower jaws work with a see-saw action, so that while one half holds the prey the other is pushed forward to draw the prey still farther inwards with the recurved teeth.

There are many other anatomical details in which snakes differ from lizards. Some of the more obvious are the great increase in the number of vertebrae and ribs, giving great flexibility to the body, and the elongation of the internal organs, such as the lungs. Usually the right lung is very long, extending in some water snakes to the rear end of the trunk, whereas the left lung is very small or absent altogether.

One great advantage of the elongated body is that snakes are able to swallow a large meal, take their time over digesting it and obviate the need for further hunting while doing so. After swallowing large prey, some snakes can go for months without further food.

Many snakes are venomous. They have fangs, hollow or grooved, down which poison from a modified salivary gland flows into the punctures

(Right) royal python Python regius, *also called ball python from its habit of rolling into ball with its head at the centre*

(Below right) horned viper Vipera ammodytes *of southern Europe, one of several species in the Old World to be given this common name*

(Below) carpet snake Morelia argus—*a constricting snake native to Australia*

made by the fangs in the victim's skin. This immobilizes the prey, but the poison also has an effect on enemies, and therefore functions as protection for the snake.

It is not surprising, after what has been said about a burrowing origin for snakes, that two of the most primitive families of modern snakes should be habitual burrowers. They are the blind snakes (Typhlopidae) and the thread snakes (Leptotyphlopidae) both of which are confined almost entirely to the Tropics. Both retain vestiges of hind limbs. The blind snakes are seldom more than 20 cm long, although a few reach 80 cm. Members of both families are blind, the eye being degenerate and covered by large scales. The skull is strong, being needed for pushing through soft earth and the body is covered by small scales, on the underside no less than on the back. Their food is insects, especially termites.

The Aniliidae or pipe snakes, the Uropeltidae or shield-tailed snakes and the Xenopeltidae or sunbeam snakes are all burrowing types and have similar characteristics to those of blind snakes and thread snakes. They eat larger prey, however, including lizards and other snakes, and some species eat eels. It is not unusual for these small primitive snakes, some of which have skeletons very like the earliest known fossil snakes, to consume prey as large as themselves.

All these are non-venomous as are the boas and pythons (family Boidae) which also have vestiges of the hind limbs. Boas and pythons kill by constriction and it is not unusual to read how one of these large snakes wraps itself around the body of its victim and slowly crushes it to death. The truth is less dramatic even if the ultimate fate of the victim is no less certain. The snake seizes its prey with the mouth and at the same time throws several coils of its body around its victim and tightens them. This restricts its breathing and it probably stops the heart as well. In any event death is by asphyxiation rather than crushing.

Boas and pythons used to be classified in two separate families because pythons are found only in the Old World and boas mainly in the New World. Moreover, python females lay eggs whereas boa females give birth to living young. There is one other difference—boas lack a supra-orbital bone in the skull. Today, these differences are not considered sufficient to maintain the two separate families, and boas and pythons are both included in the family Boidae.

This family contains some of the world's largest snakes, including the anaconda *Eunectes murinus* of northern South America, and interest is apt to centre on how large this snake grows. There have been claims for anacondas 13 m long,

European viper, the adder Vipera berus: *the zig-zag line down its back shows it to be a venomous snake*

Rhinoceros viper, of the forests of West Africa, with its tongue extended

and one for as much as 26 m. Some years ago the New York Zoological Society offered 5,000 dollars for an anaconda 10 m long, but the money was never claimed.

There is an initial difficulty in assessing records of lengths of snakes. First, the size of a moving animal is always difficult to judge. Secondly, a dead snake stretches so easily that merely laying it out to be measured may cause an increase in its length. In a small snake this increase can be nearly 50 per cent for one freshly killed. With this proviso the current record for an anaconda could be quoted as 11·4 m shot by Roberto Lamon on the banks of the Upper Orinoco in 1944; although the record cannot be substantiated, for the snake, being only maimed, recovered and disappeared.

Probably the best known member of the family is the boa constrictor (the scientific name of which used to be *Constrictor constrictor* but is now *Boa constrictor*). It lives in a variety of habitats, from semi-desert to rain forest, in South and Central America, including the Lesser Antilles. Many stories have been told about its size, the maximum for which stands at 5·5 m, making it the fifth largest snake in the world.

The second largest snake is the reticulated python *Python reticulatus,* of south-eastern Asia to the Philippines. The record length of 10 m is claimed for one shot on the island of Celebes, in Indonesia, in 1912. These are only three of the 80 species of boas and pythons. Lengths of the others are more modest.

Another aspect dear to record-makers is the weight of animals swallowed by the larger snakes. An anaconda 7 m long killed in Guyana contained a collared peccary weighing just over 45 kg and Gustav Lederer, in 1944, claimed to have induced a reticulated python 7·3 m long to swallow a pig weighing 56·6 kg. It is believed by some scientists that the African rock python *Python sebae,* 9 m long, might be able to 'stomach' a prey in excess of 68 kg.

The most venomous snakes are contained within the family Viperidae, indeed 'viper' is almost synonymous with extremes in virulent poisoning. Vipers are confined to the Old World. They range in size from Orsini's viper *Vipera ursini,* of southern Europe, 30 cm long, to the Gabon viper *Bitis gabonica,* 2 m long. Vipers are mainly ground-living, but a few climb into trees and those that do have prehensile tails for wrapping round and holding on to a branch. The mole vipers of Africa are burrowers.

Vipers have a stocky body and a very short tail.

In snakes the tail is always short compared with the body, which is one way in which they differ from lizards, but vipers' tails are even shorter than in most other snakes. Another feature of vipers is the broad, often almost triangular head, the extra room being needed to house the large venom glands. In addition the poison fangs themselves are long, in the largest Gabon vipers they measure 50 mm. Consequently, when the mouth is shut the fangs are folded back since otherwise the mouth could not accommodate them. In the small mole vipers the fangs are so long relative to the size of the head that they need to be folded onto the outside of the lower jaw when the mouth is closed.

The hunting method of vipers, essential in heavy-bodied snakes lacking speed, is to lie in wait for prey which is mainly small mammals, lizards and frogs. When the prey approaches, the viper lifts its head and strikes, then waits for the prey to die, after which the snake follows its trail by the scent, and swallows it. This has led to the idea that a snake hypnotizes its victims. People have seen a snake, immobile and watchful, near a mouse that appears unable to move. In fact, the mouse cannot move because, having received an injection of venom, it is paralysed. Depending on the kind of snake, its size, and on the amount of venom received, the prey will die in anything from a few seconds to half a minute. Since vipers lie in wait to kill they are mainly camouflaged by their colours and the broken patterns in which these are arranged. The Gabon viper is an outstanding example.

The best-known viper and the one that has given the name to the family, is the common or European viper *Vipera berus*. It ranges across Europe and Asia, from Great Britain to Japan. An alternative name in Britain is the adder. The maximum length recorded is 95 cm, but it is seldom more than 54 cm long. Adders are dark in colour with a zig-zag black line running along the back and a black V or X on the head. They spend the winter in holes in the ground or in burrows made by other animals, often in tangled masses of up to several dozens. They emerge from their winter torpor in March, and then can be seen basking by day on logs or sunny banks, especially the females.

In mating, which takes place in April, the male passes his chin, with the tongue flickering, along the back of the female, from the rear forwards as far as the head. He vibrates his body against hers, which remains passive, and he then loops his body around hers and coupling takes place. In August and September the female gives birth to

109

Puff adder Bitis arietans *with young. The snake's open mouth reveals the tongue drawn into its sheath*

(Right) Gabon viper
Bitis gabonica *of*
Africa has a gaudy
colouring but is
virtually invisible among
dead leaves on the forest
floor

(Above) scarlet king snake Lampropeltis doliata, harmless except to other snakes but often confused with the venomous coral snakes

(Left) copperhead or upland moccasin Agkistrodon mokasen is a pit viper, a rattlesnake without a rattle

live young, 6 to 20 in number and 15 to 20 cm long.

Territorial fights are occasionally observed among male adders and these are known as adder dances. Two males draw close together, raise the fore-part of their bodies and sway rhythmically, sometimes appearing to push each other. Little is known of the significance of this or of the results achieved.

Adders are feared out of proportion to the harm they inflict. One of the simplest ways of stopping people from trespassing on private land is to put up a notice 'Beware of Adders'. The ruse is effective even when the land is low-lying damp meadow, where adders do not normally live. Their typical habitat is dry, sandy soil. This snake rarely inflicts a fatal strike, although the results may be distressing. Only seven fatal encounters were recorded in Great Britain in 50 years, four of which involved children. The effect of the venom varies with the amount injected and the size of the recipient. A mouse struck by an adder will die within 30 seconds whereas a child receiving the same dose will merely be ill.

An ancient legend has it that, on the approach of an intruder a brood of baby adders will disappear into the mouth of the mother. There is every reason to doubt the story but it is of interest to note that the same phenomenon has been reported in North America for garter snakes, rattlesnakes and others.

There are five more species of viper in southern Europe, and many more in Africa, where there are mole vipers, puff adders, tree vipers, horned

vipers and others. The common viper of the Indian subcontinent to south-eastern Asia is Russell's viper *V. russelli*. It is a handsome snake with bold reddish-brown spots, outlined with black and again with white and arranged in three rows along the back and flanks. It is probably the most feared snake in that region, where children going barefooted are vulnerable to its strikes.

The puff adders include Peringuey's adder *Bitis peringueyi* which vies with Orsini's viper for the honour of being the smallest of the Viperidae; it reaches barely 30 cm in length. The largest is the Gabon viper which, with other puff adders, is strikingly but cryptically coloured in geometric patterns. The most numerous and widely distributed is the typical puff adder *B. arietans*, brown to grey with crescentic yellow markings on the back. The rhinoceros viper *B. rhinoceros*, more vividly coloured than the Gabon viper, is named for a pair of pointed and erectile, horn-like scales on the end of the snout. The venom of the puff adder is a nerve-poison and it also breaks down the blood, a potent venom slow to act but apt to be fatal to humans.

In the deserts of North Africa and south-western Asia live the horned vipers *Cerastes cerastes* and *C. cornutus*. They have a thorn-like scale over each eye, and travel over sand by a movement known as side-winding, which is found also in unrelated desert snakes in North America. Progress is achieved by throwing the body sideways, in an action difficult to describe simply, but which leaves parallel marks in the sand.

The family Elapidae contains a concentration of well-known venomous snakes, the coral snakes, the taipan, the tiger snake, cobras, kraits, the king cobra and mambas. The largest is the king cobra *Ophiophagus hannah* which feeds entirely on other snakes. It is usually about 4 m long but there are reasonably reliable records of 5 m and 6 m. Among the smaller elapids are the insect-eating snakes of Australia with very weak venom, one of which is known as the bandy-bandy, being boldly ringed with black and yellow. Its venom is, to humans, no worse than that from the sting of a wasp, whose colours it bears.

Black, red and yellow, as monochromes or in combination, are colours commonly met in animals that carry a venom or sting, or are unpleasant or unpalatable for other reasons. They are, therefore, warning colours, and almost instinctively, certainly after one experience, predatory animals tend to leave them alone; indeed all animals are inclined to give them a wide berth.

Good examples of these warning colours are found in the coral snakes of America, such as the

Arizona coral snake *Micruroides euryxanthus,* which is ringed with alternating black, yellow and red bands. Coral snakes range from this region southwards to northern Argentina. The largest is the Brazilian coral snake *Micrurus spixi,* 1·5 m long. Other species of *Micrurus* are remarkable for having a short, blunt tail that looks like a second head. When alarmed the snake hides its head beneath the coils of the body, raises its head-like tail and moves it from side to side, so that it looks like a head about to strike. Presumably this is a device, like the lizard's trick of casting its tail, that puts a less essential part of the animal in jeopardy for the greater security of the more vital part.

This seems an almost unnecessary ruse, since coral snakes have a dangerous venom and also advertise it by their colouring, but this ruse is used by a number of other snakes elsewhere. As to the warning colours themselves, their effectiveness can be gauged from the fact that certain non-venomous snakes also wear them, presumably gaining advantage from looking like the venomous ones. They are called false coral snakes and they belong to the Aniliidae, a completely different family. What is even more remarkable is that both coral snakes and their harmless mimics, the false coral snakes, tend to

be secretive. As they are often burrowers or nocturnal, their camouflage and other protective devices would seem to have a minimal value.

The taipan *Oxyuranus scutellatus* of northern Australia is probably the world's deadliest snake. It is a slender snake with a very broad head, brown above, creamy below and is up to 3·4 m long. Normally secretive it becomes aggressive when attacked and its venom affects the nerve centres controlling heart and lungs. Because its fangs are large it probably injects a larger dose than the tiger snake *Notechis scutatus* of southern Australia, which is supposed to have the most powerful venom. So it is doubtful which of the two is the most dangerous. In fact, this is largely academic for anyone who is struck by either of these snakes. The tiger snake, which is usually only 1·2 m long although it may reach 2·1 m, is heavy-bodied, grey, brown and reddish to black, with yellow cross stripes. It has been estimated that it carries enough venom to kill 387 sheep.

Some snakes of south-eastern Asia of the genus *Maticora* (also known as coral snakes) have such large venom glands that they extend backwards into the body for about a third of its length, the heart being displaced backwards to make room for them.

The cobras of Africa and southern Asia have at least as bad a reputation as some of those already discussed, and they are perhaps more dangerous because of their aggressive nature. Cobras have broad heads behind which the body is flattened and supported by long ribs. This is the so-called hood. Cobras are mainly nocturnal, with a wide diet including lizards, other snakes, frogs, rodents, birds, eggs and locusts. The reaction of a cobra is to raise its head, spread its hood and strike, even moving forward towards an intruder to do so.

The spitting cobras include the ringhals *Hemachatus haemachatus* of South Africa. They can eject their venom a distance of several metres. Should it enter the eyes temporary or even permanent blindness may result. Although the action is called spitting, it is due to compression of the venom gland driving out a trickle which is then carried on a blast of exhaled air.

Mambas are slender snakes often found in trees in southern Africa but some of them live on the ground. The black mamba *Dendroaspis polylepis* is especially dangerous. It may reach a length of 4·3 m and will strike at any sudden movement. The eastern green mamba *D. angusticeps* and the western green mamba *D. viridis* of East and West Africa respectively live in forests, in trees, often beside rivers. They feed mainly on rats and squirrels.

115

European grass snake
Natrix natrix *with its*
eggs

The kraits are highly venomous snakes of south-eastern Asia, feeding on other snakes, but their strike can be dangerous to humans and many deaths have been recorded from it. The banded krait *Bungarus fasciatus*, one of the commonest, is 1·2 m long and banded in pale yellow and black – warning colours.

The family Elapidae also includes the sea snakes of the Indo-Pacific. Most of them live in the shallow seas, only one of them being found far from land. A few come ashore to lay eggs but most bear living young and are entirely aquatic. A sea snake has a small head and the front half of the body is slender. The tail is flattened and oar-like, and is used with a sculling action in swimming. Sea snakes feed on fishes. Their venom is extremely potent and fishermen who land these snakes in their nets are particularly vulnerable to being bitten. Luckily for swimmers, a sea snake will turn and swim away at the slightest disturbance.

Pit vipers are very like true vipers in appearance. The one feature which sets pit vipers apart from all other snakes is that they have a pit on each side of the head between the eye and the nostril. It is more conspicuous than the nostril, and noticeable enough in some localities for the pit vipers to be called 'four nostrils'.

Each of the pits is double, there being a cavity in front and another behind with its separate entrance hidden just in front of the eye, and between the two is a membrane highly sensitive to changes in temperature. Each double pit is in fact a radiant heat-detector.

Although the pit vipers as a group eat a wide variety of small animals, they prey principally on warm-blooded animals, because they can pick up their trails with the two heat-detectors on their face. The thin membrane in the pit is packed with temperature-receptors, 500 to 1,500 per sq. mm. The receptors are so sensitive that they can respond to changes of 0·002°C. They enable a pit viper to detect objects 0·1°C warmer or cooler than the surrounding air, such as the warmth of the human hand held 30 cm from the snake's head. A pit viper 'sees' with its pits.

Pit vipers include the well known rattlesnakes as well as the bushmaster, copperhead and water moccasin of America, and the Asiatic pit vipers. The Himalayan pit viper *Agkistrodon himalayanus* lives as high up as 5,000 m, sometimes being found at the foot of glaciers.

The largest of the pit vipers is the South American bushmaster *Lachesis muta*, 4 m long, grey and brown with large diamond markings along the back. It has large venom glands and unusually long fangs.

European grass snake
Natrix natrix *shamming
dead. It sometimes
embellishes this macabre
display by writhing in
mock death throes*

The copperhead *A. contortrix,* 1 m long, is brown with hour-glass markings. The water moccasin *A. piscivorus* or cottonmouth, up to 1·6 m long, is slate black to olive or tan with faint brown bands. It readily takes to water and finds its food there.

Another well known pit viper is the fer-de-lance *Bothrops atrox,* which ranges from Mexico to northern South America as well as some of the Caribbean islands. Its home is in the forests, especially where there is running water, and as the forests have been cleared it has made itself at ease in the banana and sugar plantations which have replaced them, and it has at times been a considerable nuisance to those working the plantations. The name is from the shape of the head which is like that of a lance. The fer-de-lance has the habit of vibrating its tail vigorously against the ground to deter enemies, behaviour clearly linking it with the rattlesnakes. In fact, it would take little more than the formation of a rattle on the tail of a fer-de-lance to convert it to a rattlesnake.

The rattle is something that has caught the imagination even of those too far away ever to have seen a rattlesnake. It is a simple device, simply arrived at. The baby rattlesnake starts with a button at the end of its tail. In time it sheds its skin, or strictly speaking its cuticle, made of similar material to finger nails, but the piece next to the button remains. The cuticle is shed three or four times a year and each time another piece is left behind, fitting like a thimble into the previous piece. The separate pieces knock against each other when the tail is vibrated, giving the slightly blurred sound that nobody has so far adequately described except by comparing it with the hiss of escaping steam or the rapid crackling of frying fat, or even the distant sound of the old-fashioned police rattle.

One of the most common of the 80 species of rattlesnakes is *Crotalus horridus,* of the eastern United States. Despite its name it is one of the more gentle of the rattlers. In the southeast the diamondback rattler *C. adamanteus* is one of the more dangerous.

The final family of snakes, the Colubridae, is admitted by even the most knowledgeable specialists to present such a tangle that they have difficulty in sorting them out satisfactorily.

Egg of a grass snake hatching. The baby snake slits the parchment shell with its egg-tooth, which is shed soon after

There are 1,800 species in the family and they range from non-venomous to venomous. They have different kinds of teeth, their habits are variable and there are even some that use constriction to overcome prey. The most that can be done here is therefore to consider some of the outstanding members of the family: the grass snake, bull snake, egg-eating, fishing, garter, hog-nosed and a few other species.

The colubrids form the bulk of the snake faunas of all continents except Australia. Most of them are harmless to humans, and an illustration of this is found in the grass snake of Europe and the hog-nosed snake of North America, both of which seek protection by feigning death.

In the grass snake *Natrix natrix* this is only the third line of defence. The first is all too readily apparent when a grass snake is picked up. It

Diced or tessellated snake Natrix tessellata *of Europe and Asia; it feeds mainly on fish*

122

gives out a secretion from cloacal glands that produces a highly unpleasant smell. The next line of defence is that the snake strikes at the hand with the same lunge of the head as a venomous snake would use, but with the mouth closed. The third stage, when these two have failed to deter, is that the snake shams dead.

The hog-nosed snake *Heterodon platyrhinos,* before shamming dead, tries bluster. It blows itself up, hisses violently and opens its mouth widely as if about to strike. Only when these ruses fail does it sham dead. The snake quickly flips over onto its back and becomes rigid with the body slightly distorted. The mouth opens with the jaws a little awry and the tongue lolls out of the mouth. Pick the snake up and it remains rigid. Put it down on the ground the right way up and the snake immediately flips over onto its back and adopts the attitude of death, complete with rigor mortis. This feint is very convincing in grass and hog-nosed snakes.

Bull snakes are common non-venomous snakes of North and Central America where the western bull snake *Pituophis catenifer* and others are important for their destruction of pocket gophers, ground squirrels, rats and mice. Up to 2 m long, with brown diamond markings on a beige ground colour, the bull snake vibrates the tail, and if it is among dry leaves, the sound is like that made by a rattlesnake. At the same time as it rattles its tail a bull snake makes a whirring noise in the throat, which has been compared with the bellowing of a bull. On the front of the glottis (the valve that closes the throat during swallowing) the bull snake has an extra flap. When the snake forces air past this it vibrates like the reed in a wind instrument.

The egg-eating snakes *Dasypeltis,* of which there are five species in Africa, can swallow eggs whole, crush them and regurgitate the shell. They are able to do this because their teeth are very small and their mouth is even more flexible and has a wider gape than in other snakes. The neck muscles are strong and spines on some of the vertebrae project down and pierce the wall of the gullet. These spines project forward slightly, piercing the eggshell as the strong muscles contract to squash the egg. An egg-eating snake can cope with eggs twice the diameter of the body. In the initial stages of swallowing, the egg

(Above right) little whip snake Denisonia flagellum *of Australia belongs to the Elapidae*

(Right) green whip snake Coluber viridiflavus *of Europe feeds on lizards, snakes and mice*

(Far right) yellow rat snake Elaphe obsoleta quadrivirgata, *equally at home in trees and on the ground; it climbs by slipping the keeled scales on its underside into crevices in the bark*

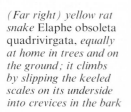

completely fills the mouth which is stretched tightly around it. A snake can still breathe while engulfing large prey like this. The windpipe can be pushed out of the mouth and withdrawn while the snake is feeding and its walls are strengthened by rings of gristle that prevent it collapsing under pressure.

The only other snake similarly adapted to eating eggs is a rare species that lives in India. But many other snakes are accused of eating eggs, some of them on no firmer ground than that they are sometimes seen in poultry roosts. Probably most of them wandered in searching for rats or a chicken.

A number of other snakes are accused of taking milk from cows, which seems highly unlikely having regard to the anatomy of their mouth. The belief is, however, widespread throughout the world.

Two species in North America, *Lampropeltis doliata* and *Atractus latifrons* are known as milk snakes. These two snakes mimic coral snakes in their colouring, although they are harmless.

Closely related to the milk snakes, are the king snakes, also *Lampropeltis*. They are brown with yellow spots and are named for their dominance over other snakes. The largest is *L. getulus* of the eastern United States, which is 2 m long. King snakes are non-venomous; they eat rodents, lizards and more especially, small snakes, including rattlesnakes to whose poison they are immune.

Another snake with the trick of shamming dead is the fishing snake *Herpeton tentaculatum,* of south-eastern Asia, from China to New Guinea and Australia. It is 77 cm long, usually reddish-brown with dark cross stripes that are white at the edges. It seems to be equally at home in fresh and salt water and can stay submerged closing its nostrils and bringing the glottis forward to seal the inner openings of the nostrils. The fishing snake is also called the board snake, tentacled snake or Siamese swamp snake. The first of these three names refers to its habit of hooking its tail around a water plant, and then stiffening its body like a board. It will also stiffen when handled, and this with the colour of the body, makes it look like the stem of a water plant. It is therefore not so much shamming dead as using its natural trick to try to hide.

The fishing snake has two small tentacles on its head. These are muscular and movable. It was thought that they were used as lures, to bring fish near the mouth to be snapped up. Recent observations suggest this is incorrect and that the tentacles merely enhance the plant-like appearance of the snake when it is stiff so that the fish have no hesitation in swimming close to it.

Unusual among the Colubridae, the boomslang *Dispholidus typus,* an African tree snake, long, slender and green, is one to be avoided by humans. It is one of the rear-fanged snakes, so called because the poison fangs are in the back of the mouth instead of in the front. It preys especially on chameleons but also eats frogs, birds and eggs. In pursuit of the two last it enters birds' nests and is a potential danger to anyone examining a bird's nest in search of food or as an ornithologist. When in danger it confronts its enemy, blowing out its neck to expose vivid patches of colour. At the same time it sticks out its tongue, holding it vertically upwards. Some rattlesnakes use their tongue in this way but after holding it vertically upwards for a while they then hold it vertically downwards.

Ribbon snake
Thamnophis sauritus *is related to the North American garter snakes; this snake swims well and often dives deep when alarmed*

*e snake, (Oxybelis)
Mexico and other
ts of tropical America*

Among the Colubridae there are many other kinds of water snakes and fishing snakes, tree snakes and vine snakes, earthworm-eating snakes, snakes that eat slugs and snakes that burrow. Among the tree snakes are the mock vipers *Psammodynastes,* small rear-fanged snakes that hang from twigs overhanging water, waiting for frogs.

So it is possible to say that the many species of snakes living today have, between them, exploited almost every kind of habitat on land, and that some have taken to living in freshwater or even in the sea. One, the house snake *Boaedon lineatum,* of Africa, has become commensal with man, living in or near houses, in thatch, under mats or in rubbish heaps. Another, the flying snake of Asia, *Chrysopelea ornata* has done its best to make use of the air. The flying snake is

also known as the golden tree snake, a name which helps identify it as to colour and habitat. The snake does not truly fly, it only glides. It launches itself from a tree, keeping the body rigid, and can fall obliquely and at a reduced speed. It does this by spreading its ribs as widely as possible and drawing up the underside to give a concave surface.

From time to time somebody tells of having seen a snake progress by leaping. The reports come from widely-separated parts of the world and putting them together we get a picture of a snake using its body as a coiled spring to bound into the air like a free-roaming jack-in-the-box. There is no proof to date that this happens. Those who tell of having seen it happen usually say that they do not expect to be believed – and usually they are not.

Selected Reading List

Barker, Will *Familiar Reptiles and Amphibians of America*, Harper & Row, New York, 1964.

Cochran, Doris M. *Living Amphibians of the World*, Hamish Hamilton, London, 1957; Doubleday, New York, 1957.

Bellairs, Angus, d'A. *The Life of Reptiles*, Weidenfeld and Nicolson, London, 1969 (two volumes).

Goin, C. J. and Goin, O. B. *Introduction to Herpetology*, Freeman, San Francisco, 1971; Freeman, Reading, Berkshire, 1971.

Loveridge, Arthur *Reptiles of the Pacific World*, Macmillan, New York, 1946.

Martens, Robert *The World of Amphibians and Reptiles*, Harrap, London, 1960.

Parker, H. W. *Snakes*, Robert Hale, London, 1963.

Pope, Clifford H. *The Giant Snakes*, Routledge & Kegan Paul, London, 1961; Knopf, New York, 1961.

Porter, K. R. *Herpetology*, Saunders, Philadelphia, 1972.

Schmidt, Karl P. and Inger, Robert F. *Living Reptiles of the World*, Hamish Hamilton, London, 1957; Doubleday, New York, 1957.

Smith, Malcolm A. *The British Amphibians and Reptiles*, Collins, London, 4th edn. 1969.

Stebbins, Robert C. *Amphibians of Western North America*, University of California Press, Berkeley and Los Angeles, 1951.

Swinton, W. E. *Fossil Amphibians and Reptiles*, British Museum (Natural History), London, 1958.

Vogel, Zdenek *Reptiles and Amphibians, their Care and Behaviour*, Studio Vista, London, 1963; Viking Press, New York, 1965.

Acknowledgments

Acknowledgments to photographs on the following pages:

2–3, 4, 6–7, 8 (top), 8 (bottom), 9, 10, 12, 13, 14 (top), 14 (bottom), 15, 17 (top), 17 (bottom), 18–19, 20, 21, 22–23, 24–25, 27, 28–29, 30, 31, 33, 36, 37 (top left), 37 (top right), 37 (bottom left), 38, 39, 40–41, 41, 42–43, 43, 46–47, 48, 55, 60, 62, 63, 68, 70–71, 72 (top), 72 (bottom), 75, 76, 76–77, 80, 88–89, 90, 91, 92–93, 94–95, 97, 98–99, 101, 102, 105 (bottom), 106–107, 116–117, 118–119, 122–123, 124: Jane Burton/Bruce Coleman. 3 (top): Oxford Scientific Films/Bruce Coleman. 10–11, 32, 34–35, 113, 115: Jack Dermid/Bruce Coleman. 19 (top), 56–57, 61, 78: S.C. Bisserot/Bruce Coleman. 19 (bottom), 50–51, 79 (bottom): James Simon/Bruce Coleman. 26–27, 47 (top), 47 (bottom), 74 (bottom): David Hughes/Bruce Coleman. 37 (bottom right): A. Grandison. 45: J. Markham/Bruce Coleman. 49 (top), 49 (bottom), 53, 54, 70 (top), 73, 86, 94 (top), 105 (top), 125, 126: John Norris Wood. 49 (bottom), 112 (bottom): L. Lee Rue/Bruce Coleman. 52: David C. Houston/Bruce Coleman. 58–59: Francisco Erize/Bruce Coleman. 64, 68–69, 101 (top), 103 (bottom): Bruce Coleman. 65: Joe Van Wormer/Bruce Coleman. 66–67, 109: Simon Trevor/Bruce Coleman. 70 (bottom): Rod Borland/Bruce Coleman. 74 (top), 127: Russ Kinne/Bruce Coleman. 79 (top): C. Walker/Natural Science Photos. 81: Peter Jackson/Bruce Coleman. 82–83, 104, 124 (top): John Brownlie/Bruce Coleman. 84–85: Vincent Serrenty/Bruce Coleman. 87 (right): John Wallis/Bruce Coleman. 96: Geoffrey Kinns/Natural Science Photos. 100: Norman Myers/Bruce Coleman. 103 (top): P. H. Ward/Natural Science Photos. 108, 112 (top): P. Boston/Natural Science Photos. 110–111: Des Bartlett/Bruce Coleman. 114 (top): A. Leutscher/Natural Science Photos. 114 (bottom): R. Weymouth/Bruce Coleman. 120–121: Peter Hinchcliffe/Bruce Coleman.

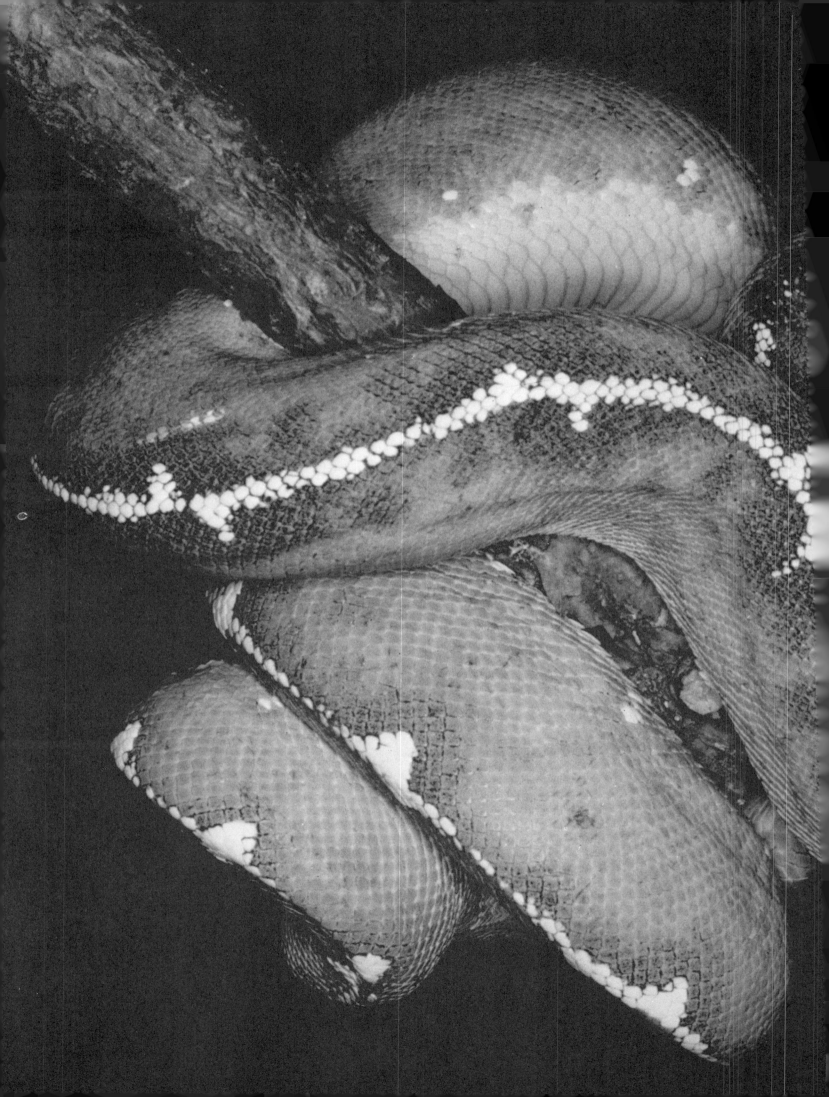